COLOUR CRAFTS

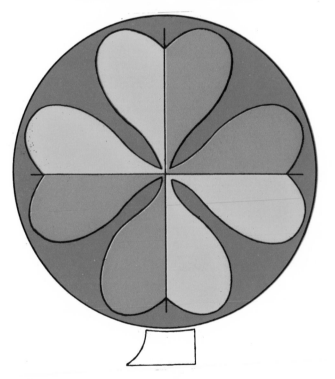

Macdonald

First published October 1969
First English edition 1970
Reprinted 1971
© 1969 Santillana, S A. de Ediciones
English translation © 1970, Macdonald & Co. (Publishers) Ltd.
St. Giles House, 49/50 Poland Street, London W1A 2LG
Printed in Spain

Novograph, S. L. Ctra. de Irún, Km. 12,450, Madrid-34

D. L.: M-14.002 - 1971

SBN 356 03523 9

Volume 3

Working with string, raffia and material

The projects in this book are divided into five grades, from very simple to advanced. The colour key below shows the grades and corresponding symbols, which are repeated at the beginning of each project for easy reference. The very simple projects are designed for younger children but the grades are only intended as a rough guide. Very young children may need some help.

 Very simple

 Easy

 Moderately easy

 More complex

 Advanced

String, raffia and material is the third volume in the *Colour Crafts* series. It tells you how to make nearly ninety models. Each project is illustrated with step-by-step colour pictures and photographs.

The colour-coded square at the beginning of each project tells you how complex each one is. If you get stuck on any model, pick another one and go back to the harder one later.

Start each project by collecting all the things you will need, which are listed at the beginning. If you cannot find one of them, see if you can think of something else you could use. You can use string instead of raffia, and if you want bright colours you can often use wool. It is harder to get an even finish with raffia, so we only suggest using it where it can be woven, stitched or wrapped round something. The book also shows how to use various kinds of material. Sometimes you will have to sew pieces of material together, but on other models you can simply glue them. The best glue for this is PVA (or any similar impact adhesive), which can also be used for all other gluing jobs in the book.

Some of the models, like toy cats and dogs, must be stuffed. We have suggested using kapok or pieces of foam rubber, but you can also use small pieces of old material, sawdust or even straw. Generally you should use whichever you can find easily.

The objects illustrated in the book are, we hope, both attractive and useful. Once you have mastered the basic techniques of handling string, raffia and material you should be able to make up your own designs too.

The measurements in this book are given in centimetres (cm) and metres (m). One centimetre is the equivalent of $\frac{3}{8}$in, but if you wish to work in feet and inches, we suggest that an easier system of conversion is to halve the measurements given in centimetres and call them inches. Thus 1cm becomes $\frac{1}{2}$in, 10cm becomes 5in and so on. Provided you follow this method consistently, you should have no difficulty in making the models.

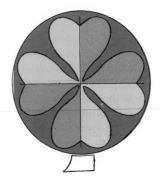

FINGER CHAIN

This kind of chain can be used in many ways. You will find some of them in this book. These chains are often made with a crochet hook. But here you can see how to make one with just your fingers.

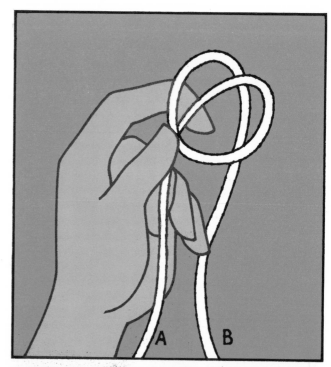

Hold a length of wool like this.

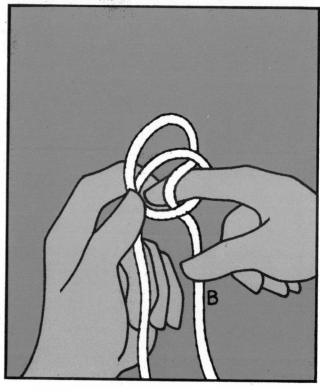

Pull B through the loop as shown.

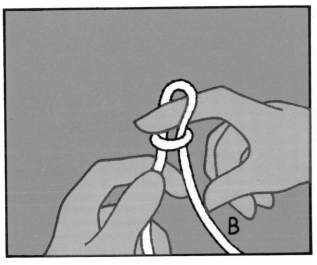 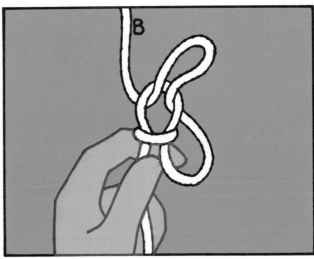

Now pull B up.

Now push B through the new loop.

You can do the same with other materials like raffia and string.

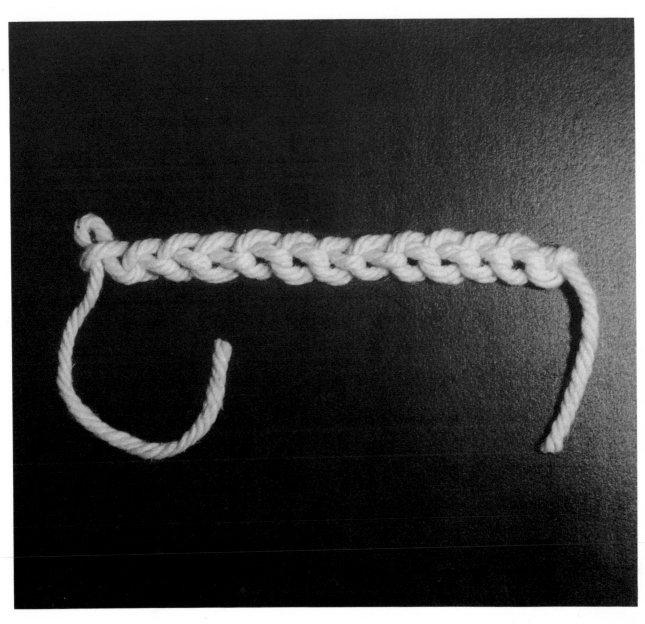

MATERIALS:

- ● **Wool**
- ● **Scissors**
- ● **Needle**

PLAITING

Cut pieces of wool of different colours. Sew the top ends together to stop them fraying and to help you plait easily.

Start plaiting with the first thread on the right, passing it alternately over and under the other threads. Do the same with the thread that now remains on the far right.

You can use this type of plaiting for covering seams and oversewing materials like hessian, canvas and linen.

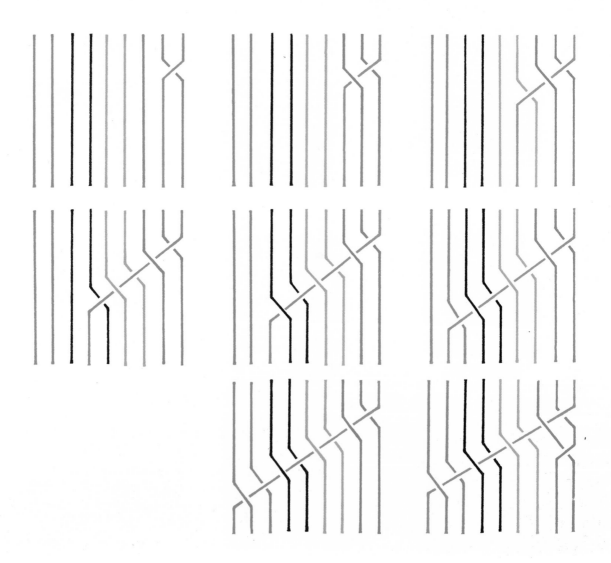

MATERIALS:

● Four pieces of string
● Pieces of wool
  in different colours
● Four little bells
● Needle and cotton
● Scissors

BELLS

Cut four pieces of string and some pieces of wool in different colours. Tie them all together with a knot.

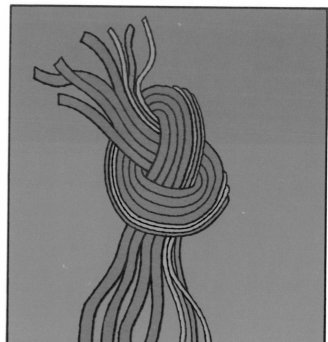

Start plaiting just below the knot. The first and the second strands are formed by two pieces of string. The third strand consists of the pieces of coloured wool.

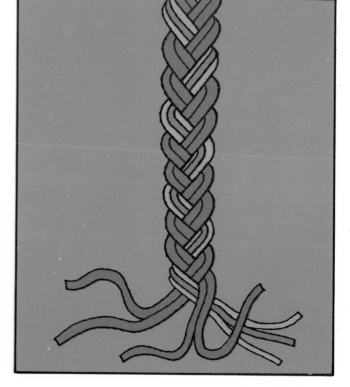

Do not plait the ends. Turn them up and tie to the bottom plait with a piece of wool as shown in the big picture. Tie a few bells or a small rattle to the bottom end.

If you hang the bells on a door, they will look nice and make a pleasant noise when the door is opened or shut.

MATERIALS:
- Material
- Felt-tip pen
- Stuffing
- Needle and cotton
- Scissors

HIPPOPOTAMUS

Cut two shapes as shown out of the material.

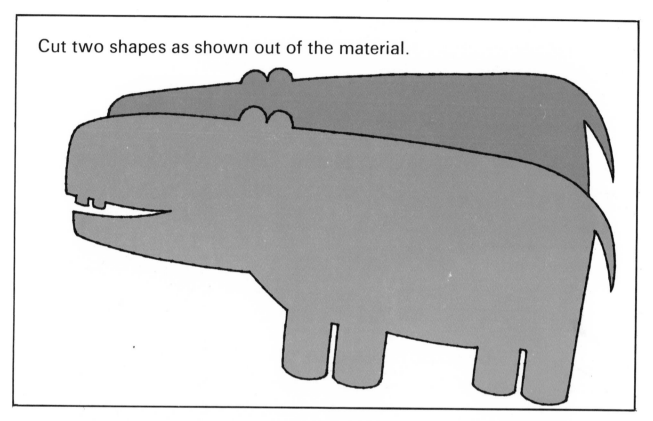

Sew together with small stitches, leaving one part unsewn. Fill the inside with sawdust, kapok or pieces of foam rubber and sew up.

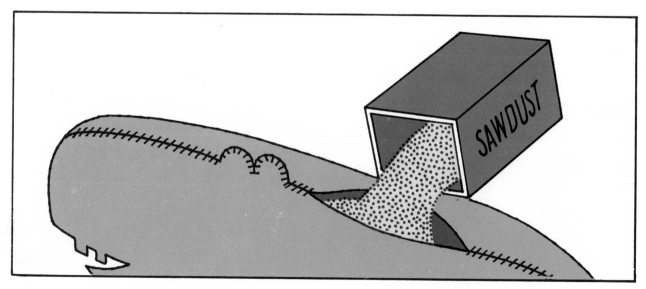

Decorate the hippopotamus with felt-tip pens or by gluing on pieces of coloured material.

WOVEN RAFFIA

Raffia is usually sold by the skein. It is best to start by making the skeins into balls to stop the raffia getting tangled

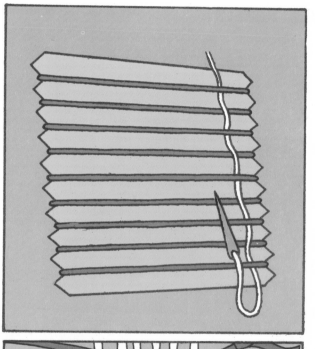

Take a piece of cardboard and cut the edges into points as shown. Wind the red raffia round the cardboard, keeping the lines straight on the front side of the cardboard. Now weave the white raffia through the red.

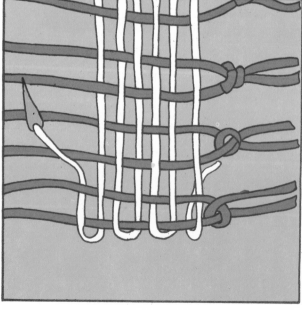

Remove the piece of cardboard by cutting the red raffia on the back side. Knot the loose ends in pairs to make fringes.

RAFFIA BRACELETS

Cut out a piece of thin card long enough to fit easily round your wrist.

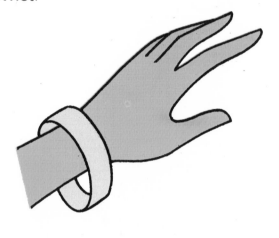

Glue the ends together.

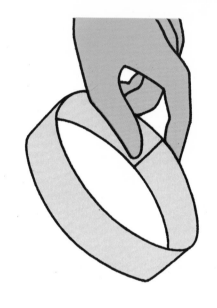

Cover the card with raffia.

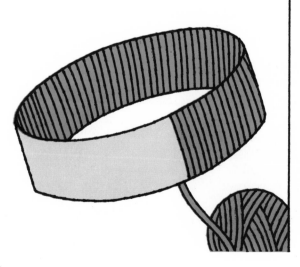

Glue the ends of the raffia to the card.

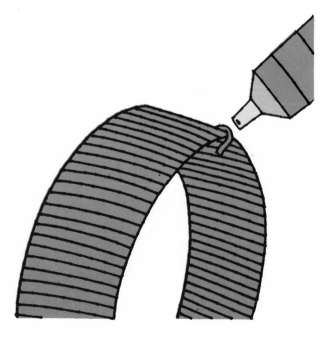

You can make other bracelets with different coloured raffia.

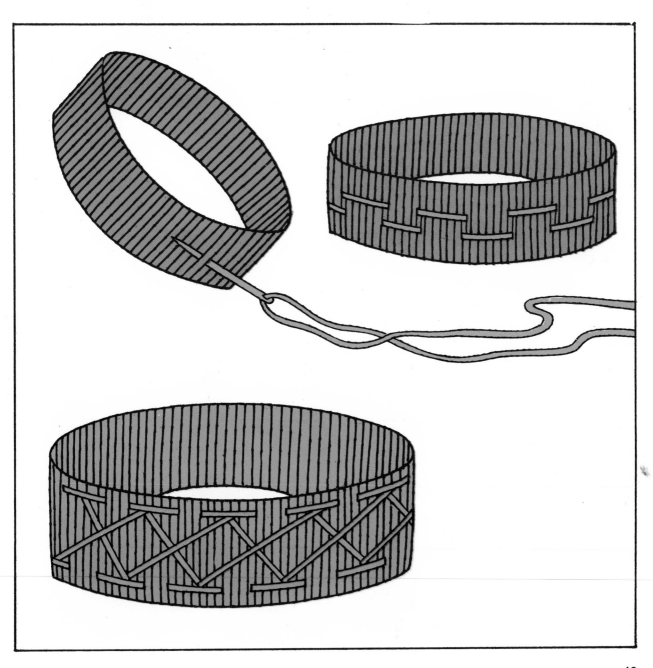

KNOTS

Being able to tie knots is useful for anything from simply tying shoelaces, to making a ladder or putting up a tent. In general, knots should be easy to tie, be strong, and easy to undo.

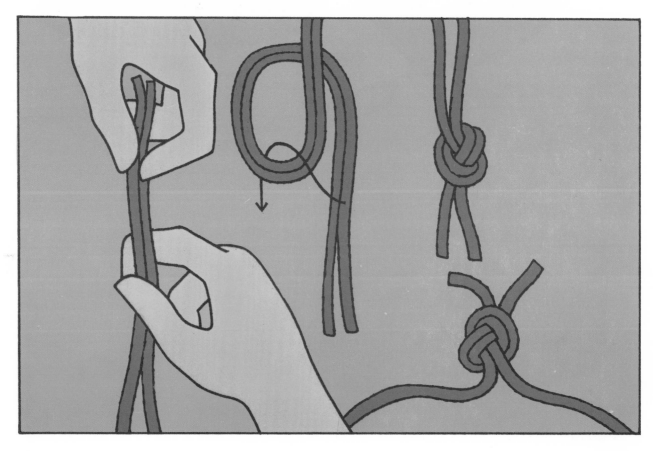

On these two pages you can see how to tie three different types of knots.

WOOL DOLL

Cut several pieces of thick wool and tie the ends together (fig 1)
Continue tying them as shown in figures 2, 3 and 4.

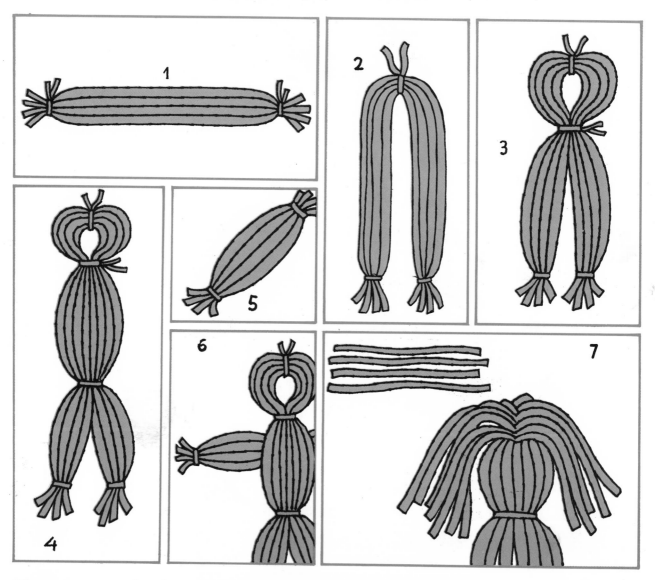

Tie more strands of wool as in figure 5 and pass these through the body to make arms (fig 6).

Sew some shorter pieces of wool on to the head to make hair (fig 7).

22

RINGS ON FELT

Draw a pattern on a piece of paper and trace it on to the felt.

Sew the rings and hooks on to the felt, following the pattern.

Make up other patterns, combining rings etc in different ways.

You can make curtains, belts, flags etc. in this way.

If you want to make the pattern in the picture, cut out the felt as shown in the big picture.

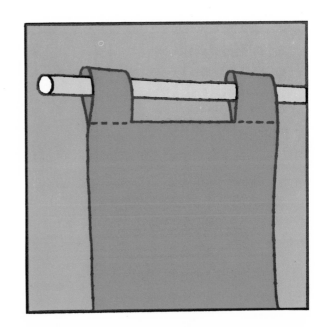

Fold over the two ends that stick out, and stitch along the dotted lines.
This makes loops for a curtain rod or flag pole.

MATERIALS:
● **Different coloured felt**
● **Scissors**
● **Paper and pencil**
● **Needle and cotton**
● **Tailor's chalk**
● **Stuffing**

BALL

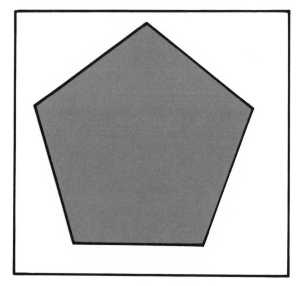

Draw a five-sided pattern on a piece of paper as shown in the picture. Cut it out. Place it on each piece of felt and draw round the edge of the paper pattern with the chalk. Cut twelve identical shapes out of the felt.

Sew the pieces together like this. Leave one piece open. Turn the ball inside out so that the seams do not show.

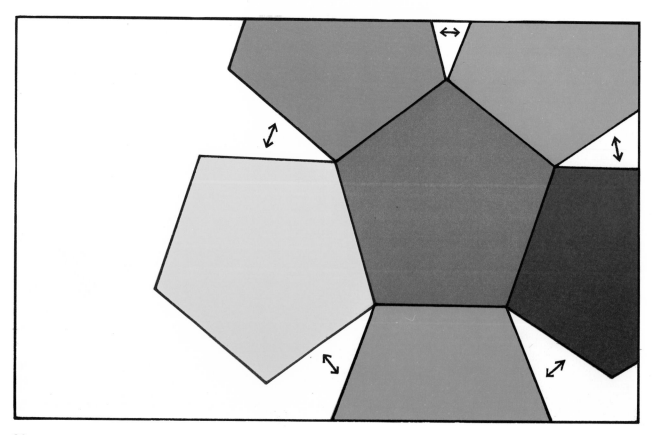

Stuff the ball with kapok or foam rubber and sew up the side you left open.

MATERIALS:

- **Material**
- **Kapok or foam rubber**
- **Emerald blue, brown and orange acrylic paint**
- **Scissors**
- **Paint brush**
- **Strands of brown wool**
- **Needle and cotton**

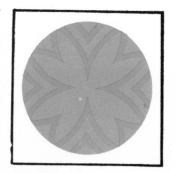

DOLL

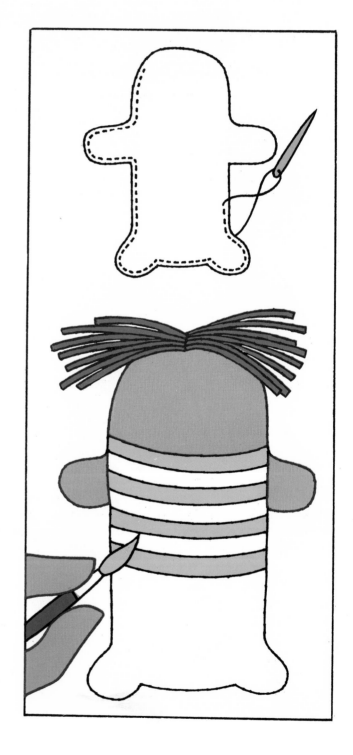

Cut out two shapes like this from the material. The bigger they are the more attractive the doll will be.

Sew the pieces together, leaving a small opening.

Turn the material inside out so that the seams do not show.

Fill with sawdust or wool and then sew up the opening you left. with very small stitches.

Cut some strands of brown wool. Sew them to the centre of the head with very close stitches. The strands of wool should be loose and fall untidily either side of the head.

This doll was decorated with acrylic paint, but you could use felt-tip pens instead.

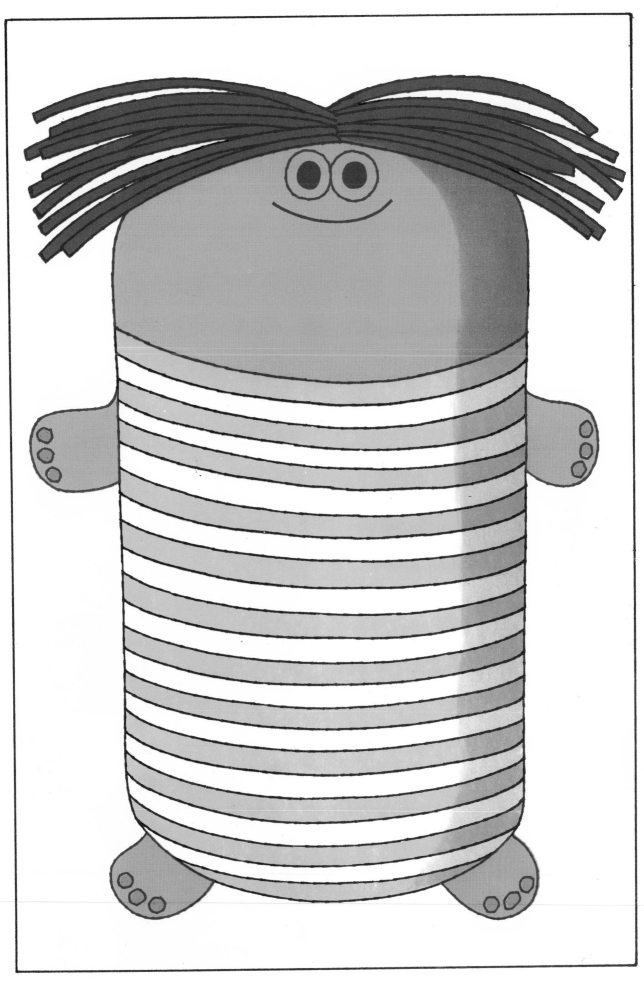

29

MATERIALS:
- **Material**
- **Stuffing**
- **Needle and cotton**
- **Felt-tip pens**
- **Scissors**

MONK

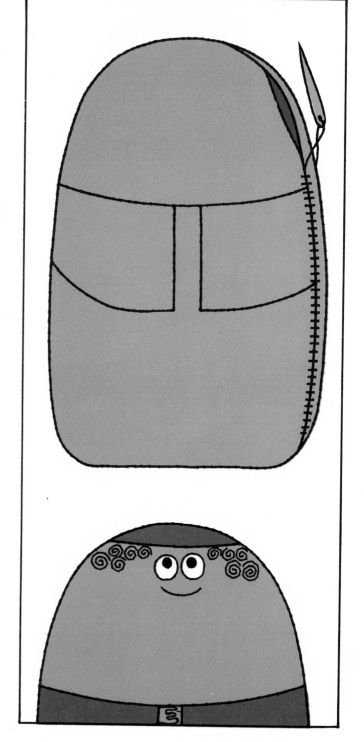

Take the material and cut out two shapes as shown in any size you like.

Sew them together but leave an opening so that you can stuff the doll with kapok or foam rubber.

When you have done this, sew up the opening.

Draw in the eyes, nose, mouth and hands, and colour the rest of the doll with thick felt-tip pens.

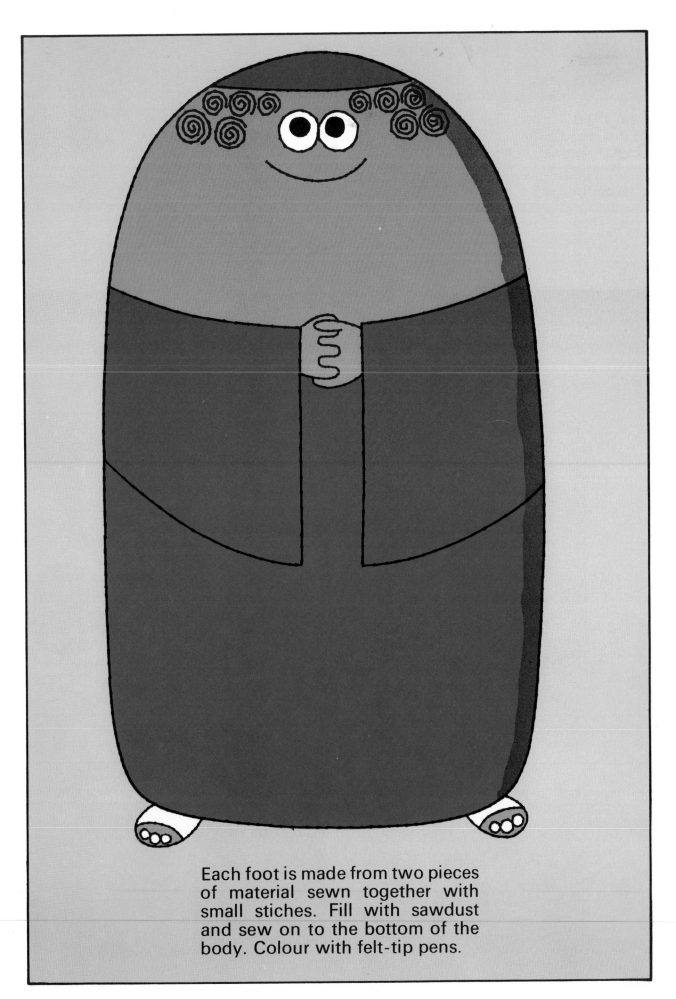

Each foot is made from two pieces of material sewn together with small stiches. Fill with sawdust and sew on to the bottom of the body. Colour with felt-tip pens.

DECORATED TINS

A good way to keep your pens, pencils and brushes tidy is to put them in tins.

Here you can see how to decorate old tins from the kitchen.

One way is to wrap wool round a tin, sticking it down with glue. Another way is to cut out a piece of felt the same length as the tin and stick it round the outside. You can put another piece inside.

MATERIALS:

- Plastic sponge
- Coloured felt
- Glue and a brush
- Scissors
- Wire
- Thread

LITTLE BIRD

Tie a ribbon round the sponge to divide it into the head and body.

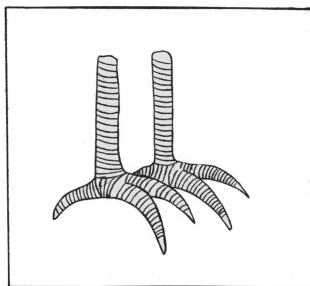

The feet are made of wire covered with thread. Fix these underneath the bird's body.

The eyes, beak and feathers are made from different coloured pieces of felt and are glued or stitched to the head and the body.

PARROT

GLUE

Make this parrot in the same way as the little bird on the previous page.

Use different colours and shapes, as this is a different bird.

You can use this method to make any birds you like.

MATERIALS:
● Checked
   material
● Grey, black,
   red and white
   material
● Stuffing
● Needle and
   cotton
● Scissors

DOG

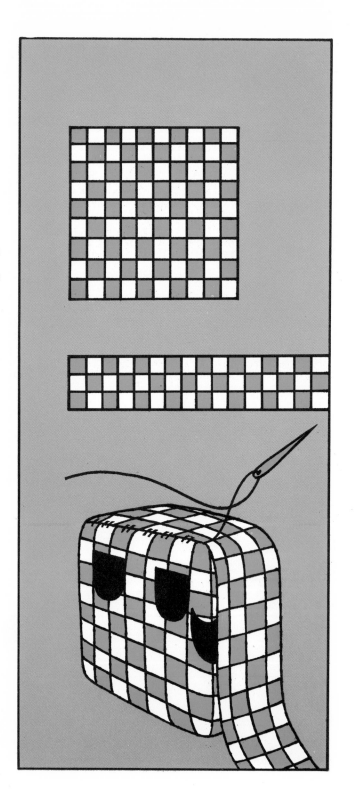

Cut two equal sized squares out of checked material (the sizes of the model shown are 13cm by 13cm).

Then cut another piece of the same material 5cm by 55cm.

Decorate one of the squares to make the dog's face by sewing on the grey, black, white and red pieces of material to make eyes, mouth, eyebrows, nose and ears. Use very small stitches.

Sew the two squares to the long piece of material, leaving an opening.

Stuff the dog with kapok or foam rubber and sew up the opening.

CAT

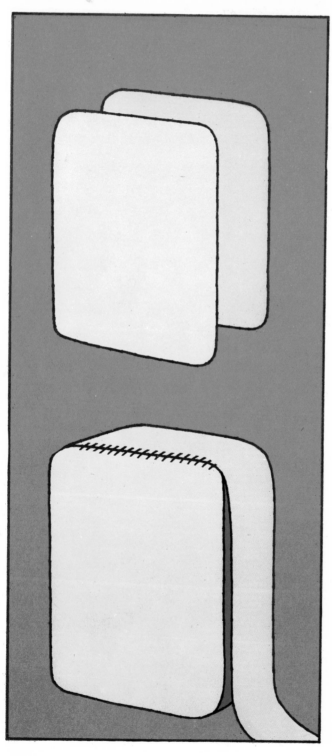

Cut out two rectangles in the material (the sizes on this model are 13cm by 18 cm).

Cut out a long piece of material 3cm by 75cm.

Sew each rectangle to the long piece. Leave an opening for stuffing with kapok or foam rubber.

Once stuffed, sew up the opening.

Paint in the eyes, eyebrows, whiskers, mouth, etc as shown.
Now decorate the body as shown.

You can use powder paints, water
colours, drawing ink or acrylic paint.

41

DOG

Cut two rectangles from the material.

Leave one part open. Turn the material out the right way.

Cut the nose, mouth, ears and feet out of felt.

Also cut a long, narrow piece, as on the two previous animals. Sew one rectangle to each side of the strip with the seams on the wrong side.
The corners should be sewn round, not square.

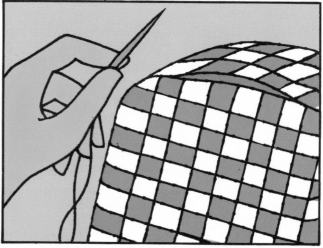

Sew these on to the body with small stitches.

Stuff the dog with kapok or foam rubber. Sew up the opening.

MATERIALS:

● Scissors
● Strip of felt
● Thick wool
● Thick crochet
  hook

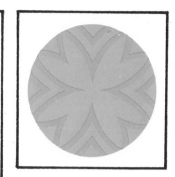

TASSELS

Take a strip of felt. Make as many dots as you can with a ballpoint pen, leaving 1cm between each dot.

Cut some pieces of wool about 30cm long.

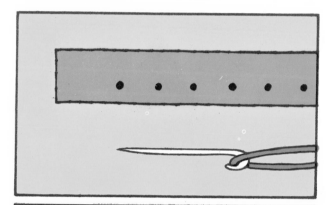

Push the point of the crochet hook through the first dot to make a hole. Pull a piece of wool through the hole with the crochet hook as shown.

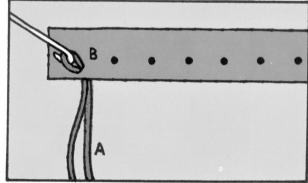

Thread the ends (A) through the loop (B). Pull A down.

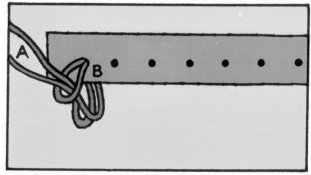

Do the same in the other holes.

When the strip is full, tie the wool
in pairs as shown.

MATERIALS:

● Cardboard
● Scissors
● Darning
  needle
● Wool

POMPOMS

You can use these pompoms to make necklaces and decorations, and in other projects in this book.

Cut two circles out of cardboard. Make a hole in the middle of each as shown.
Put one on top of the other.

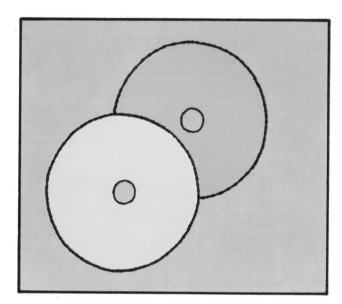

Thread through a needle the end of a ball of wool. Wind the wool round and round the cardboard ring until the cardboard is completely covered and the hole in the middle is almost closed.

Cut the wool round the outer edge of the cardboard.

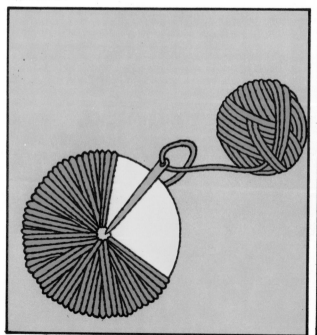

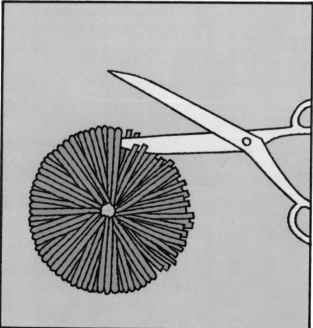

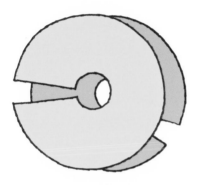

Tie the wool in the middle between the two pieces of cardboard. Now cut the cardboard and remove from the wool. Round the pompom off with your hands.

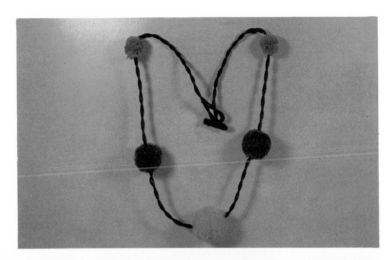

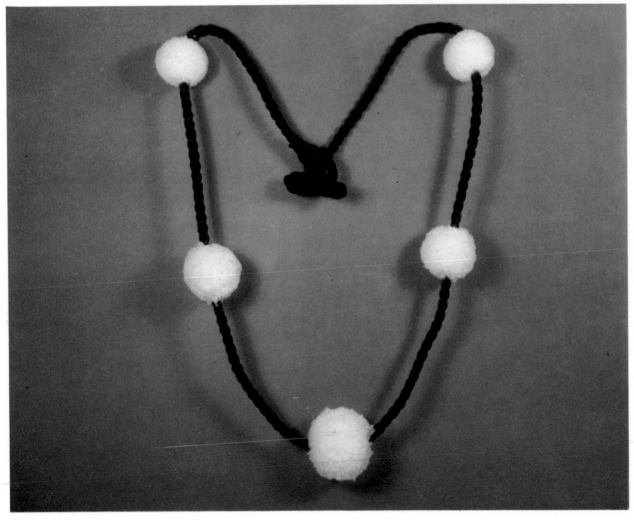

MATERIALS:

- Hessian or canvas
- Patterned material
- Orange, white, black, yellow and green material
- Needle and cotton
- Feathers, foam rubber, or other stuffing

CUSHION

The easiest way to make the cushion is to cut out two squares of sackcloth or canvas and decorate one of them with the pieces shown in the drawing.

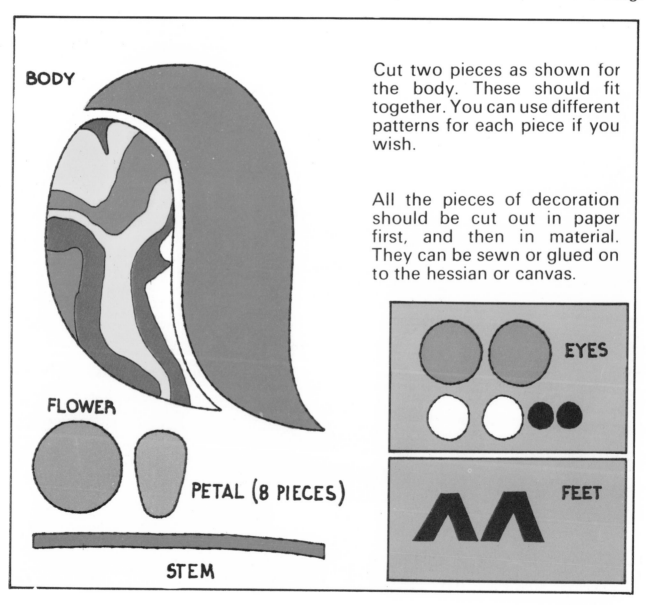

BODY

Cut two pieces as shown for the body. These should fit together. You can use different patterns for each piece if you wish.

All the pieces of decoration should be cut out in paper first, and then in material. They can be sewn or glued on to the hessian or canvas.

EYES

FLOWER

PETAL (8 PIECES)

FEET

STEM

Sew the squares together with the seam on the wrong side. Leave an opening.
Turn the cushion inside out.
Stuff with feathers, cotton wool or pieces of foam rubber. Sew up the opening.

4

FISH

This is the first of six models that you can use for decorating the doors of a cupboard.

Draw the outline of any fish you like on a piece of paper.

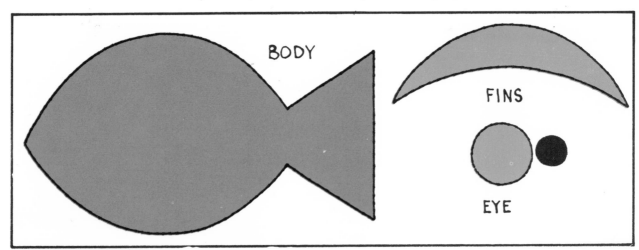

BODY

FINS

EYE

Use your paper pattern to cut the body of the fish out of red material, two fins out of green material, the large circle for the eye also out of green material, and the small circle out of black material.

Sew the body and the fins on the hessian with big stitches.

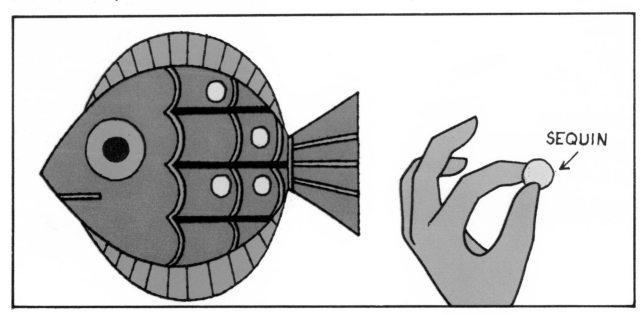

SEQUIN

Now sew on the pieces for the eye.

Decorate the fish with sequins and make scales out of black and blue wool.

BUTTERFLY

The materials used are the same as for the fish on the previous page.

Make a paper pattern.

Use the pattern for cutting the wings of the butterfly out of green material. Sew them on to the hessian.

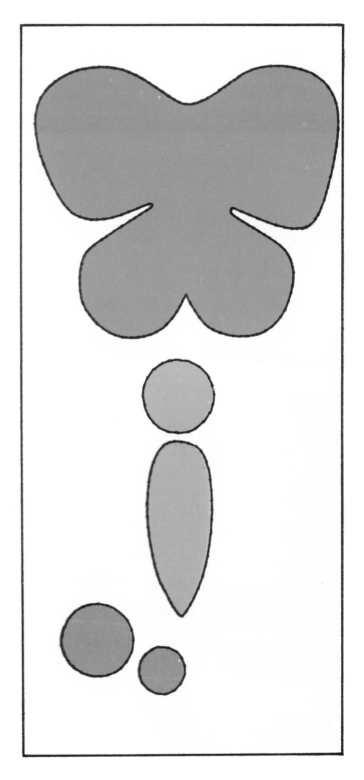

Cut the head, body and spots out of coloured materials and sew on top of the wings.

The sequins also make decorations.

Make the antennae in chain stitch.

Embroider two dots for eyes.

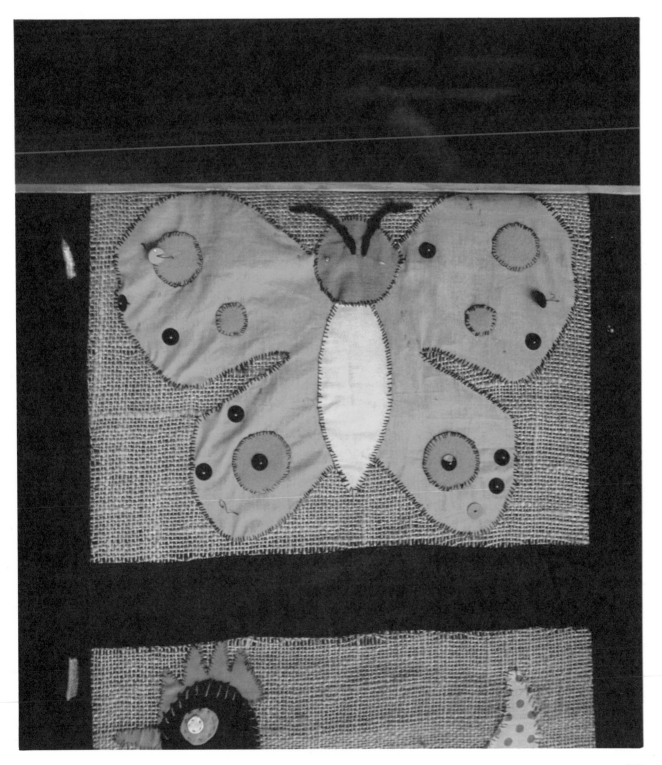

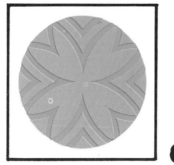

COCK

The materials are the same as for the fish and the butterfly.

Use a paper pattern to cut the body of the cock out of pink material.

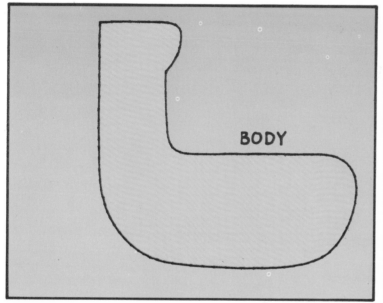

BODY

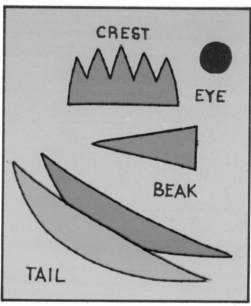

CREST

EYE

BEAK

TAIL

Sew the body of the cock on to the hessian.

Cut the other pieces out of the coloured materials.

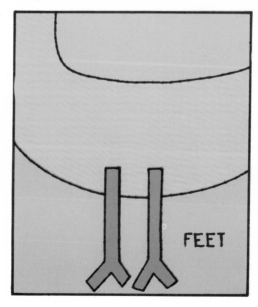

FEET

Sew the pieces on to the body and the hessian as shown.

CAT

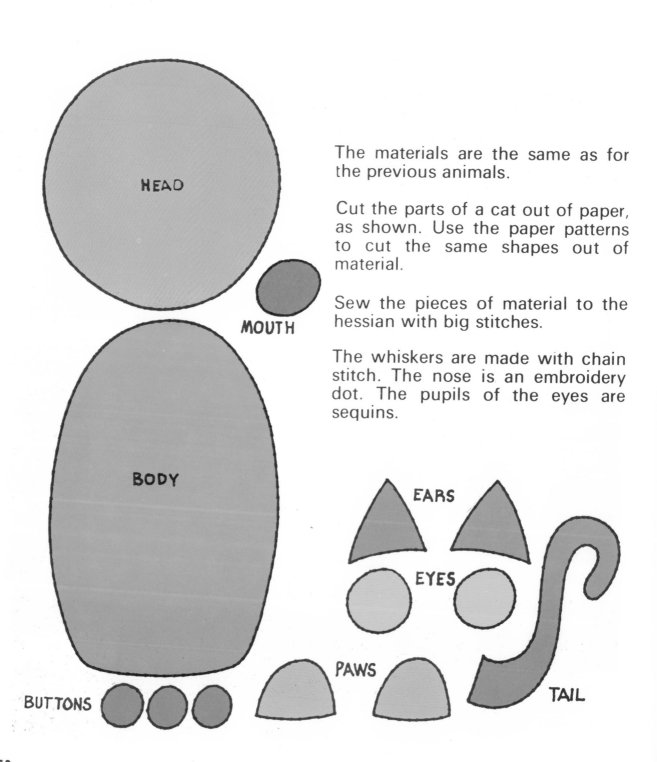

HEAD

MOUTH

BODY

The materials are the same as for the previous animals.

Cut the parts of a cat out of paper, as shown. Use the paper patterns to cut the same shapes out of material.

Sew the pieces of material to the hessian with big stitches.

The whiskers are made with chain stitch. The nose is an embroidery dot. The pupils of the eyes are sequins.

EARS

EYES

BUTTONS

PAWS

TAIL

FLOWER

Use the same materials as for the cat.

Sew the different parts of the flower on to the sackcloth.

Sew them with large stitches, using black wool.

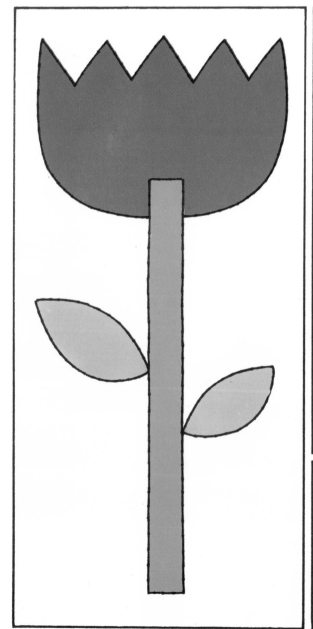

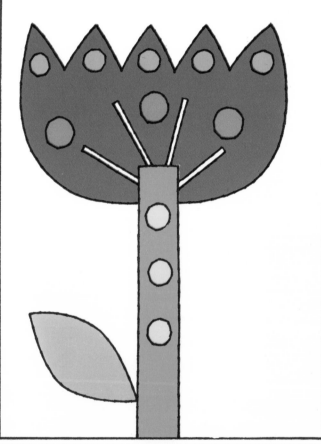

Put sequins on the stem and the flower.

You can chain stitch all round the flower with green or blue thread if you wish.

HEN

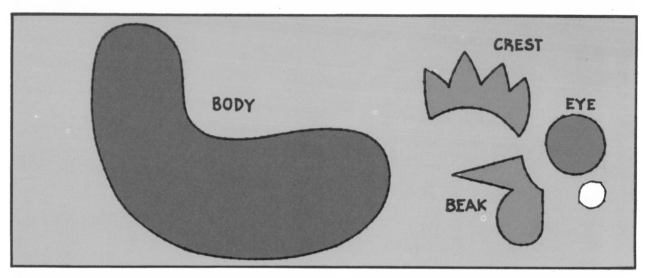

The materials needed are the same as for the previous pictures.

Cut out the hen's body, first in paper and then in material.

Sew it on to the hessian.

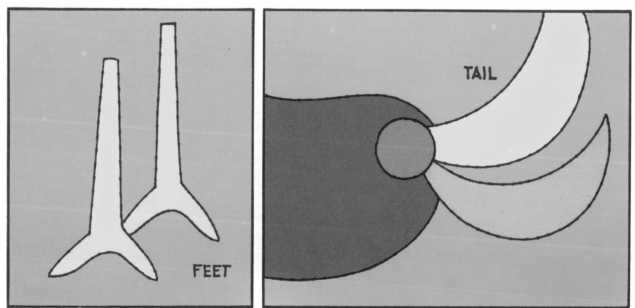

Cut the eye, crest, beak, tail and feet out of different coloured material.

Sew them into position on the body as shown.

WORKING WITH PLAITS

Plait three strands of wool of the same colour together.

Make more plaits using different coloured wool.

Sew the plaits together side by side.

You can make lots of things such as belts, rugs, dolls' bedcovers etc. in this way.

MATERIALS:

- Embroidery
  canvas
- Different
  coloured raffia
- Wool needle
- Pencil
- Scissors

RAFFIA PICTURE

Draw a picture on the embroidery canvas.

Sew the raffia on to the canvas, following your drawing.

Each straight line is only one stitch, even though it may be very long. The circles (for example the top of the tree or the centre of the sun) are done with small stitches.

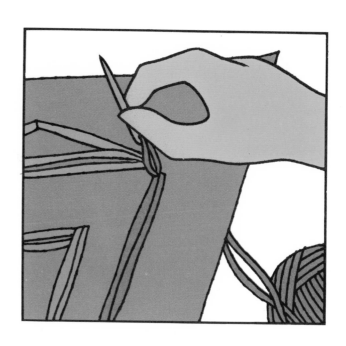

STRING FRIEZE

Cut out a piece of cardboard, as long as you like.

Make a pencil drawing on the cardboard.

Glue string along the lines of the drawing.

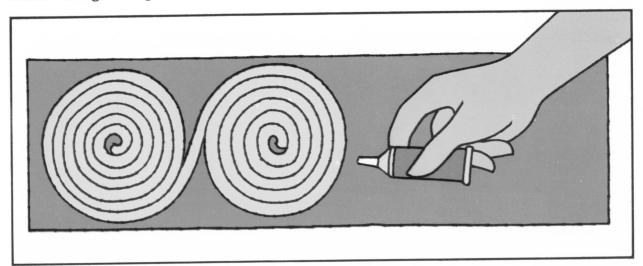

You can see three frieze patterns on these pages.

You can make up all kinds of friezes.

POUFFE

This pouffe is very easy to make. It makes an attractive ornament, or you can use it as a footrest when you are sitting down.

First make a paper pattern, any size you like.

Place the pattern on a pretty piece of material and cut round it.

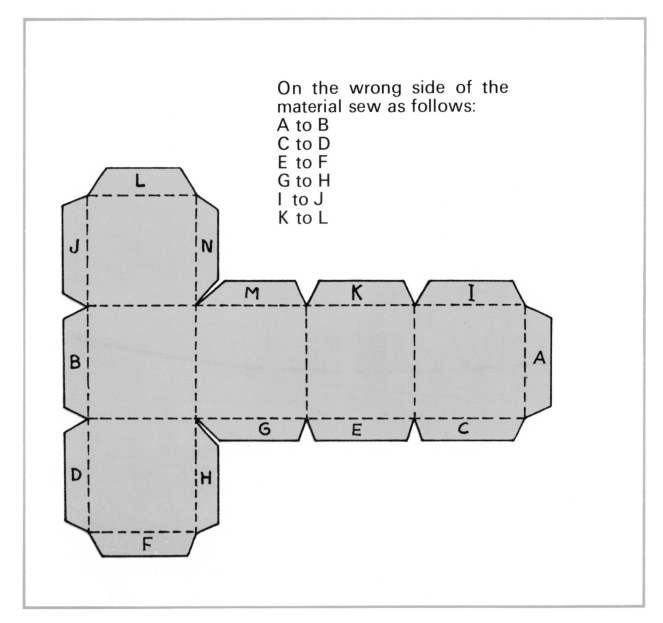

On the wrong side of the material sew as follows:
A to B
C to D
E to F
G to H
I to J
K to L

Turn the material the right way out so that the seams do not show. Fill with wool, straw or other stuffing materials. Finally, sew M to N with small stitches, using cotton the same colour as the material so that the seam will not show.

MATERIALS:
- Paper and pencil
- Needle and cotton
- Felt
- Scissors

HANDLE COVERS

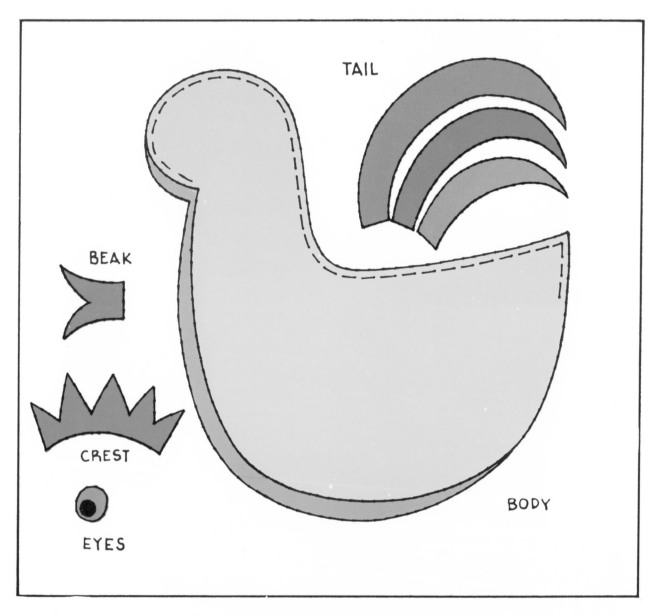

TAIL

BEAK

CREST

EYES

BODY

Cut out the patterns, first in paper and then in felt.

Put the crest, beak and feathers between the two pieces that form the body.

Sew the two body pieces together along the dotted lines.

With a little imagination, you can invent other designs for handle covers.

MATERIALS:
- Embroidery linen
- Coloured wools
- Crochet hook
- Needle and thread
- Paper and pencil

PICTURE

Copy the pattern in the big photograph on to a piece of paper and trace it on to the linen.

Make each part of the picture as follows:

STEMS: Make a chain as shown in the top picture on the right and sew it on to the linen, following the lines you have traced.

THE OUTLINE OF THE LEAVES: These are also chains sewn to the linen.

THE MIDDLES OF THE LEAVES: These are filled with large criss-cross stitches as shown in the lower drawing on the right.

FLOWER: First make a chain and join the two ends together to make a circle. Sew the circle to the material. Then make smaller and smaller circles until you have filled up the flower.

PEKINGESE

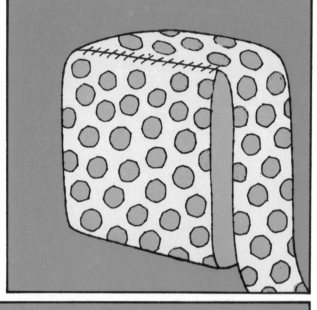

Cut two equal squares out of the printed material. The size of the model is 13cm by 13cm.

Cut a piece of material 5cm by 55cm.

Sew the pieces as shown in the drawing, leaving an opening to put in the kapok stuffing. Stuff the dog and sew up the opening.

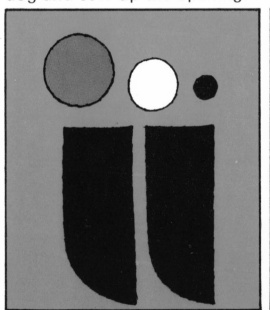

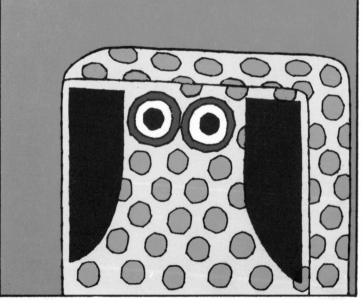

The eyes and ears are cut out of black, grey and white material and sewn on to one of the squares of printed material.

You can make as many variations as you wish, using the same method. Try to think of different ways of decorating the animal.

For example, if you add a piece of red material in the shape of a beak to the animal you have just made, he will look like a penguin, and the bits that looked like ears will now look like wings.

MOBILE

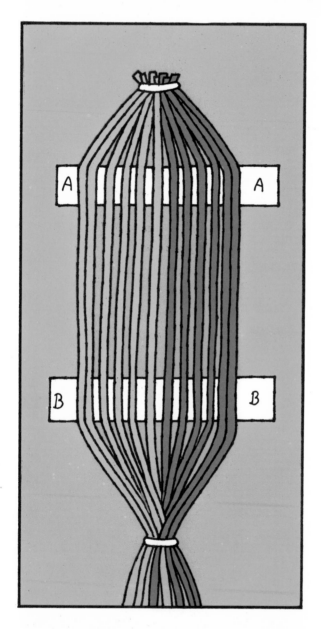

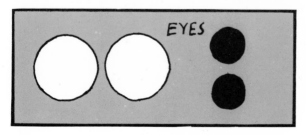

EYES

Cut out two strips of thin card.

Place them on a flat surface. The distance you leave between them depends on how long you want the fish to be (in the model shown the gap is 15cm).

Cut the green and blue wool into strands about 45cm long. Glue the green strands to the strips of card covering about half the surface. Fill in the card still showing with blue strands. Glue the strands very close together, almost on top of one another.

Glue A to A and B to B.

Tie knots at both ends of the strands for the head and the tail.

The eyes are two circles cut out of black and white felt and glued to the end which forms the head.

PLAITED WIG

Cut fairly long pieces of wool (say 1.5m long).

Place them flat, as shown, and tie them in the middle in pairs with other short pieces of wool.

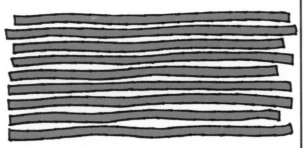

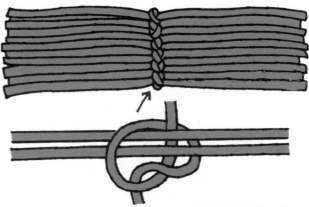

Tie a bow at the end of the plaits to stop them coming undone.

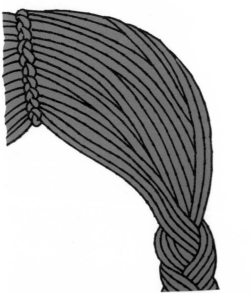

Leave a loose bit on either side of the central join and start plaiting.

RAFFIA LAMPSHADE

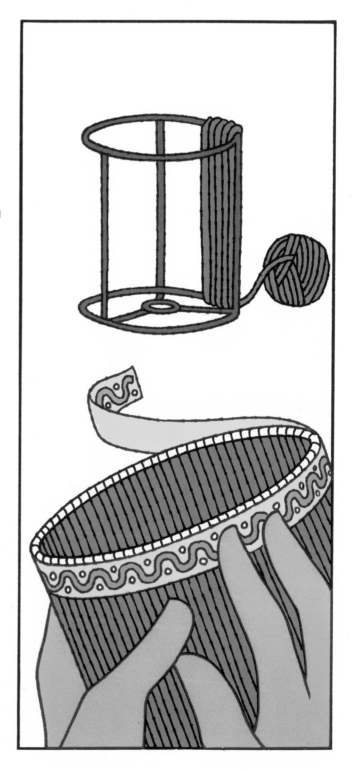

Cover the side of the frame with raffia as shown in the drawing.

Decorate the edges of the lampshade with braid trimming, sewn to the raffia with small stitches.

LITTLE
SPANISH SOLDIER

Cut out two pieces of linen the same shape as the drawing below.

Decorate one of these pieces as shown, in the following order:
1. Long stitches in thick red wool
2. Stitches in thick orange wool
3. Embroidered dots in black wool
4. Stitches in grey wool
5. Stitches in black wool

Paint spirals in orange drawing ink on the cheeks and chin. Cover the rest of the face with blue wool, using large stitches.

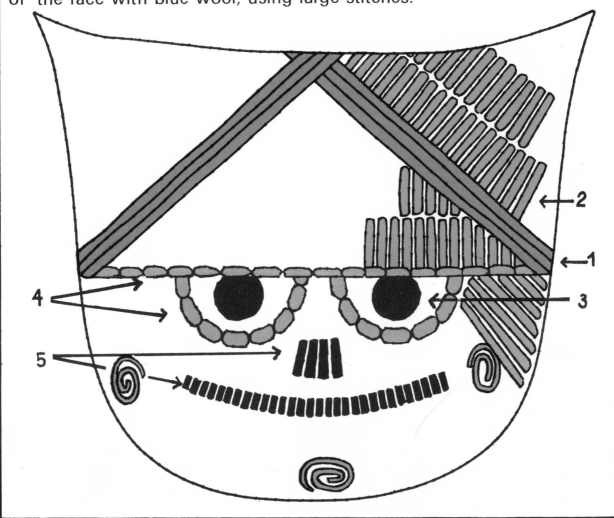

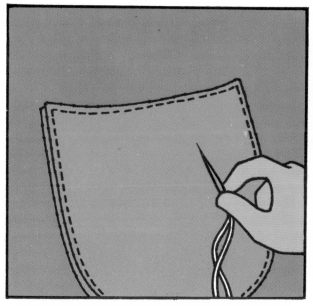 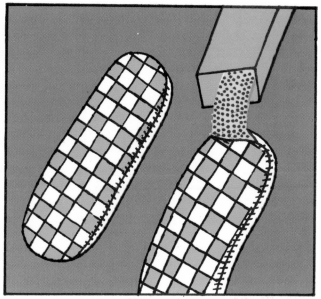

When you have finished the face, place it wrongside up on the other piece of linen that you have cut, and sew along the outside edges. Leave an opening.
Turn the material the right way out. Fill with kapok and sew up the opening.

To make the legs, cut four pieces like these from printed material. Sew together and fill with kapok. Sew them on to the bottom of the back of the head. Make two black wool tassels to finish off the cap.

FELTBOARD

A feltboard can sometimes be used instead of an ordinary blackboard. It can be used by teachers, or you can use it for playing school, memory games etc.

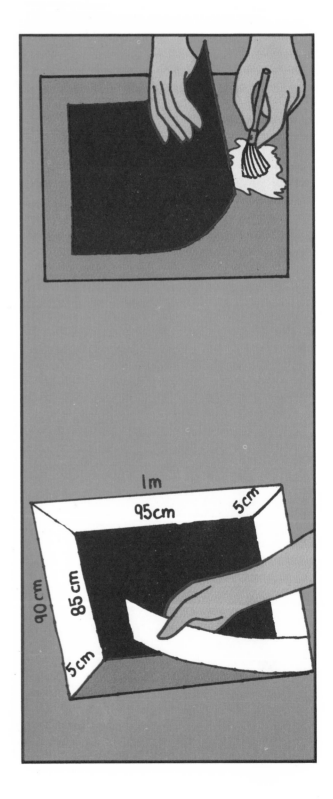

Find a board about 1m by 90cm.

Cut out a piece of black felt 90cm by 80cm. Glue this to the board, leaving a margin of 5cm on each side.

Cut two lengths of white felt 1m by 95cm by 5cm and two more 90cm by 85cm by 5cm.

Glue these lengths to the board still showing round the black felt.

Cut out objects in different coloured felts to make a picture. Use lots of different colours. You will not need glue. The objects will stick on by themselves. You can take them off again and put them in different places.

MATERIALS:

● Cardboard
● Scissors
● Glue
● Raffia

PICTURE FRAME

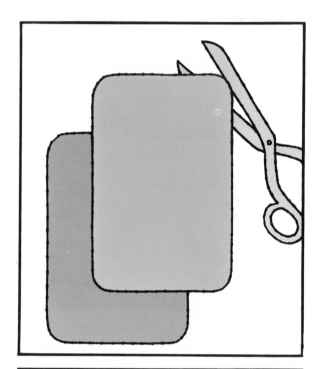

Cut out two pieces of cardboard the same size as shown.

Round off the corners.

On one of the pieces draw a line parallel to the edges. Cut out the middle along this line. Put the middle piece on one side. The outside piece is the frame.

Cover the frame with raffia as shown.

Glue the other piece of cardboard to the back of the frame.

Cut out a cardboard shape (as shown below in yellow). Bend along the dotted line.

Paste section A on to the back of the picture frame.

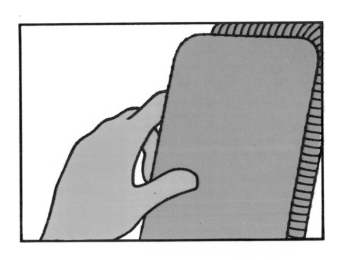

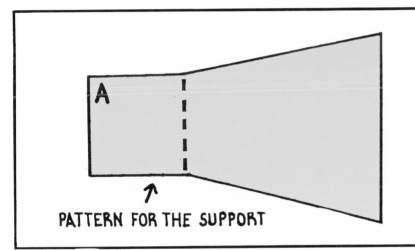

A

↑
PATTERN FOR THE SUPPORT

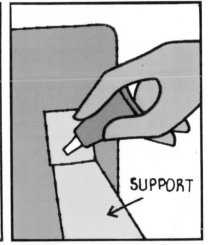

SUPPORT

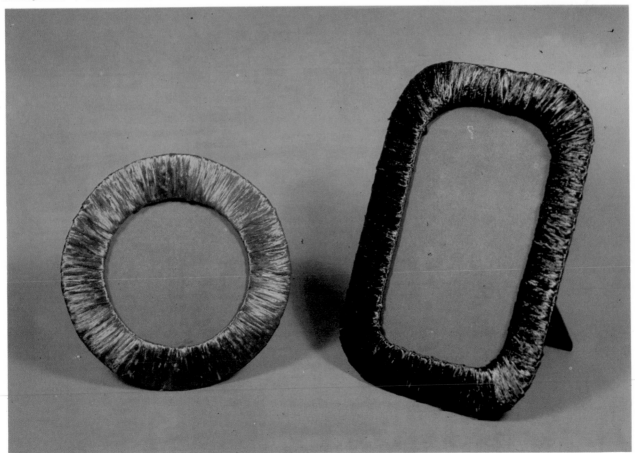

MATERIALS:

- Printed material
- Scissors
- Needle and cotton
- White, black and grey wool
- Green felt

DOLL

Cut a rectangle out of printed material for the body.

Fold in half and sew up the three sides with small stitches. Leave a small opening.

Make the face as follows:
—embroider the mouth in black wool, keeping the stitches very close together.
—make a nose out of a piece of green felt sewn on to the printed material.
—draw three circles for the eyes. Work over them with wool, using very close stitches. The pupil is a sequin.

Fill the doll with sawdust. Then sew up the opening.

The legs are twice as long as the head. Stuff them with sawdust and sew on to the bottom of the head.

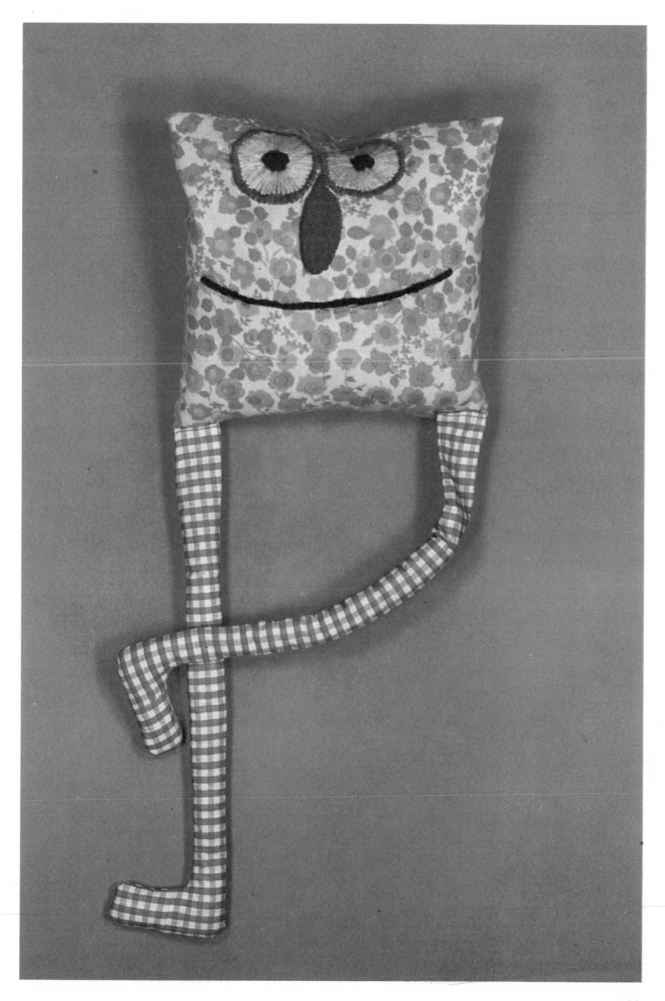

MATERIALS:

- Strips of inner tube rubber
- Thread
- Strips of material
- Coloured felt
- Needle and wool
- Scissors

BALL

First make a small ball using thin strips of rubber.

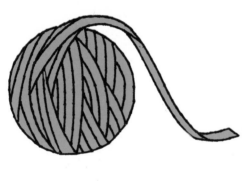

Now make the ball bigger by winding thread round the ball.

Now the ball is almost finished. Try bouncing it.

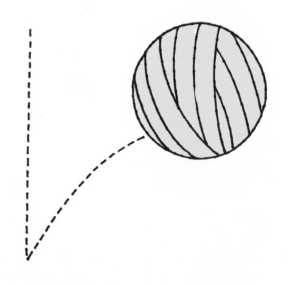

Cut long strips of material and roll them round the ball too.

Cut out a paper pattern like this one. The size will depend on the size of your ball. Use the paper pattern to cut out four pieces in different coloured felt.

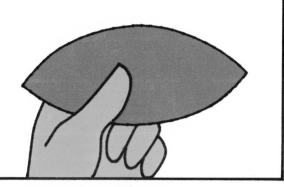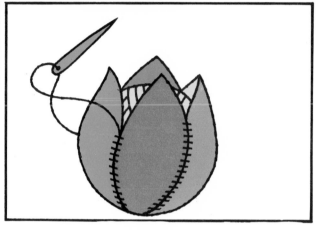

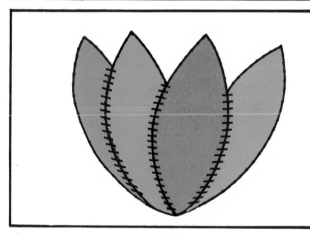

Sew them together as shown, leaving open at the top.

Put the ball inside. If necessary, add more felt pieces until the ball is completely covered.

WOOL CARPET

Draw this design in pencil on a piece of card. Choose some different coloured wools which blend together attractively.

The pencil design is filled with lengths of wool. Glue on the wool, starting at the centre of the design and working outwards until the pattern is completed.

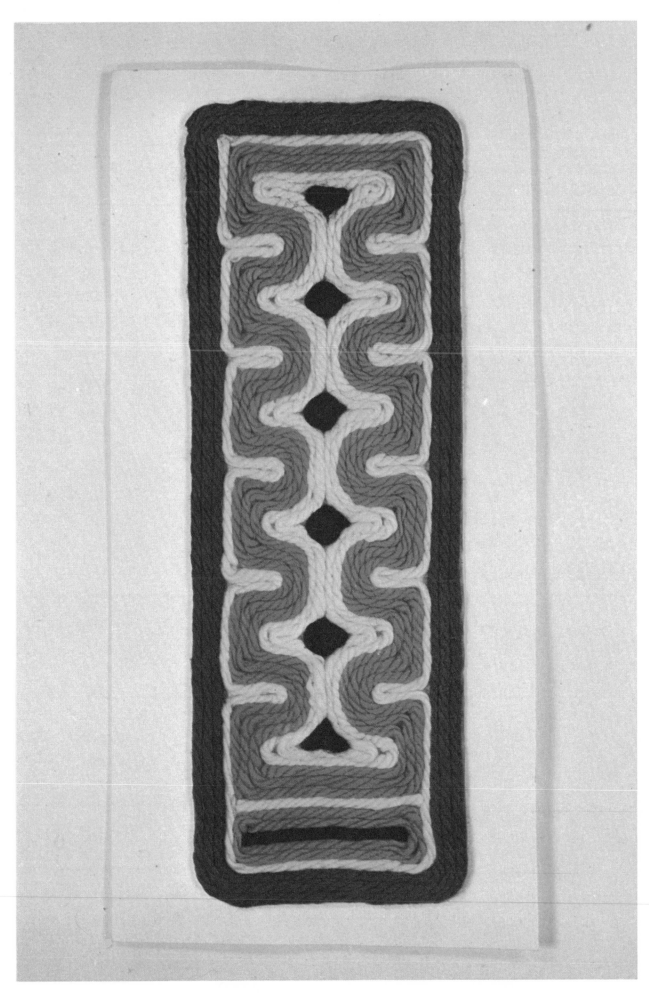

FISH MOBILE

Cut the fish shapes shown, out of embroidery canvas.

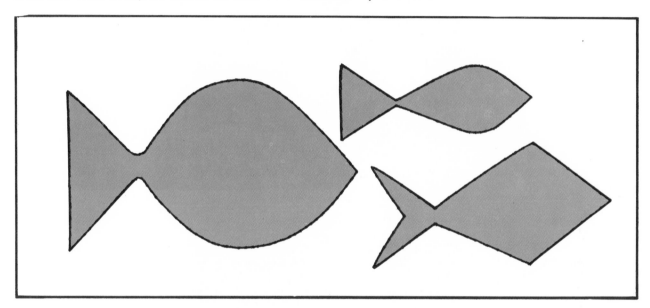

Glue the coloured ribbons round the edges of the canvas. Decorate the fishes with sequins or buttons sewn on to the body.

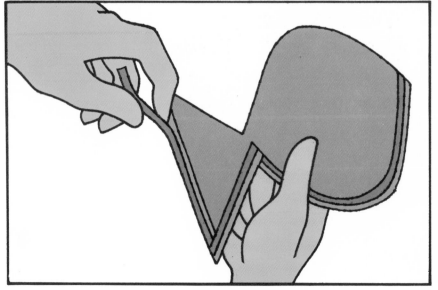

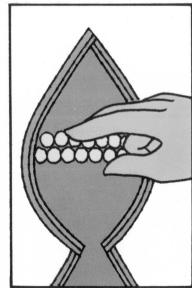

Tie one end of a piece of cotton thread to the body of each fish. Tie the other end to a strip of wood or strong cardboard.

You can invent other fish shapes or copy them from books and magazines.

FLAMINGO

Make a wire framework as shown, working down from the beak to the feet.

Make the body by threading on a pompom. You will find instructions for making pompoms on page 46.

Wrap pink wool round the neck and head as shown. The beak and feet should be covered with yellow wool.

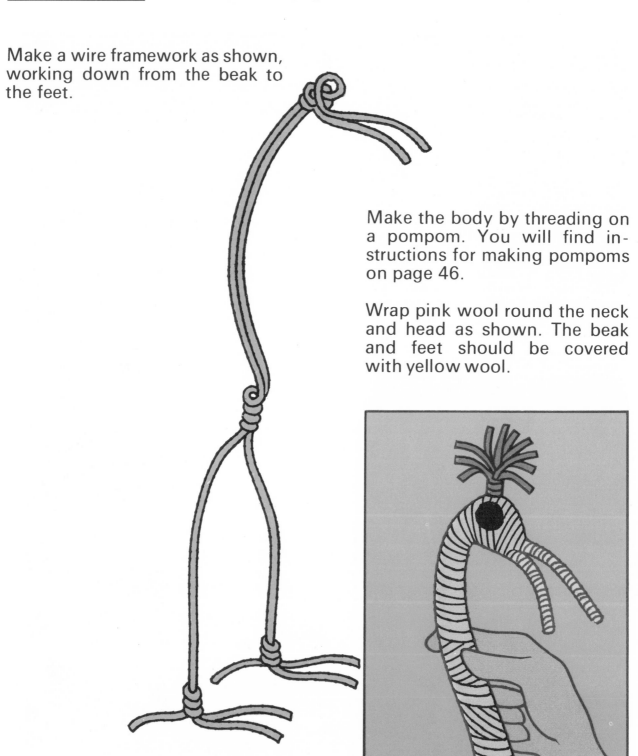

Sew on more pieces of pink wool as shown to make the crest and the tail.

You can make models of all kinds of wading birds using different frames and coloured wools.

MATERIALS:

- ● Embroidery canvas
- ● Scissors
- ● Darning needle
- ● Different coloured raffia
- ● Pencil

RAFFIA FISH

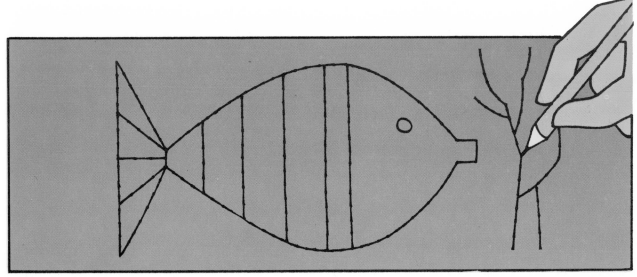

Cut out a piece of canvas as shown. Draw the design on to it.

Stitch in raffia along the lines of the drawing.

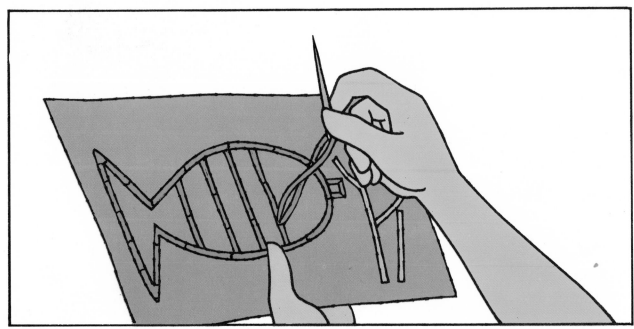

Now fill in the outline, mixing colours as you wish.

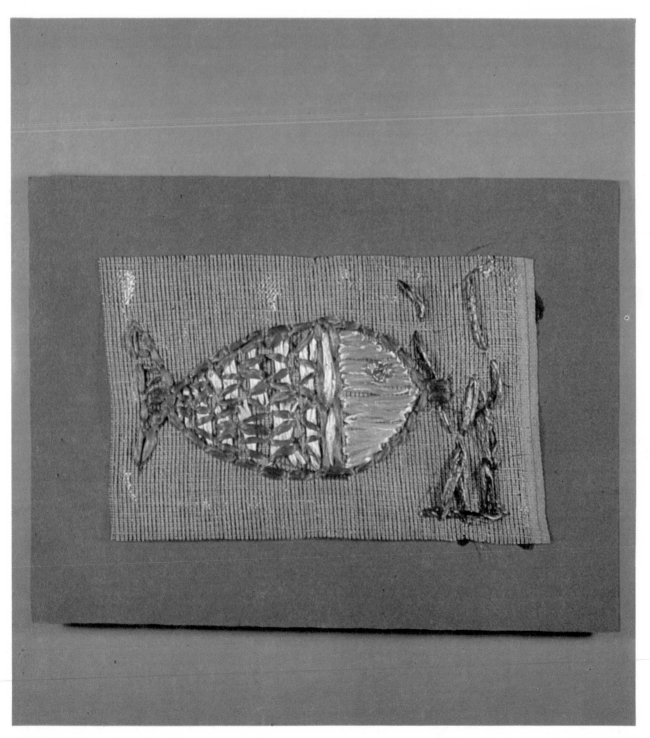

MATERIALS:

● Cardboard
● Coloured paper
● String
● Scissors
● Glue
● Pencil

TREES

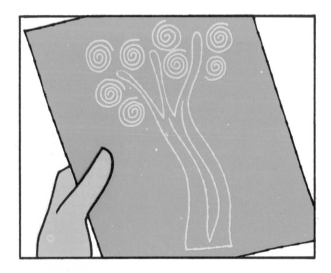

Cut a rectangle out of cardboard. Glue coloured paper on to it.

Draw a design on to the coloured paper. Fill it in by gluing down string and more pieces of coloured paper, if you wish.

CURTAIN

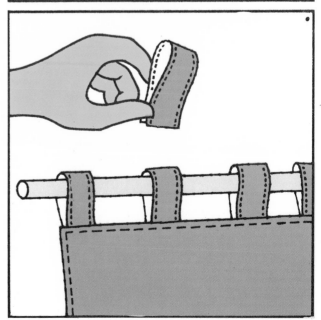

Cut a piece of hessian any size you wish.

Fold back and make a hem on each edge, as shown.

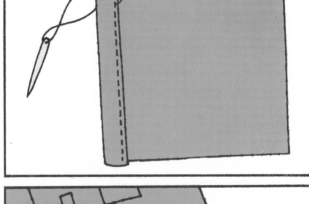

Draw a picture on a piece of paper. Trace it on to the hessian.

Fill in the drawing on the hessian by gluing on pieces of different coloured material.

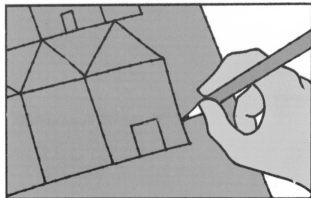

Cut long-shaped pieces of hessian as shown. Make hems on them.

Fold them in two and sew the ends on to the back of the curtain.

Hang up the curtain by pushing a rod through the hessian loops.

Try to make your room decorations bright, practical, cheap and original. This curtain is all of these things as well as being very easy to make.

GLOVE PUPPET

Draw and cut out a paper pattern in the shape of piece A. Then cut two pieces the same shape out of printed material. Sew the pieces along the dotted lines only, with the right sides together.

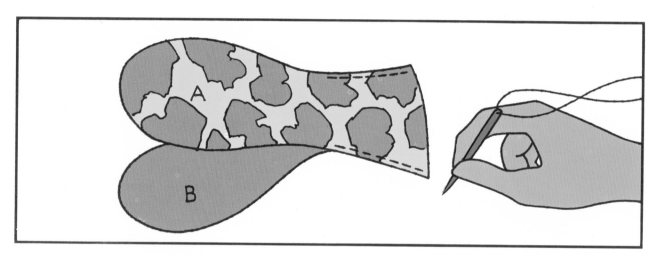

Cut the blue shape on the right out of blue material. Fold along the dotted line. Sew A to the A on the first shape, and B to B. Turn the glove the right way out.

The ears are made of the two pieces held by the hand in the drawing. Sew them on to the top of the puppet as shown in the big picture.

The eyes are made of pink and blue felt and are glued on to the puppet.

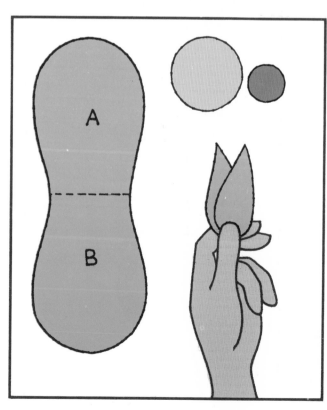

MATERIALS:

- Printed material
- Black wool
- Black felt or material
- Scissors
- Stuffing material
- Needle and cotton

DOG

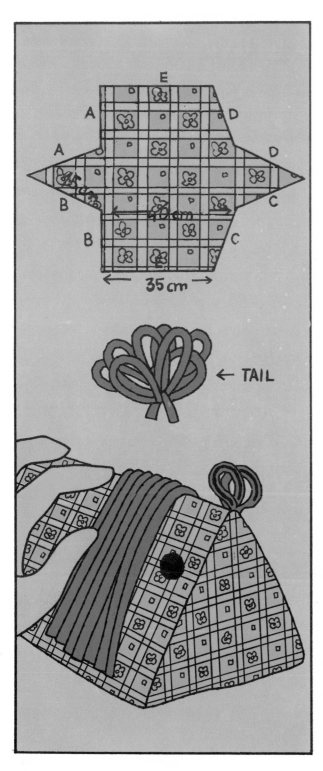

35 cm

← TAIL

Draw this pattern on to paper, using the measurements shown. Put the paper pattern over the material and cut round the edge.

Sew the material on the wrong side, sewing together the sides marked on the pattern with the same letter (i.e. A to A etc.).

Leave sides B/B unsewn. Now turn the material the right way out.

Stuff with straw, wool, etc. Sew up the opening with very small stitches.

The hair, nose and tail are made of black wool. The eyes are circles of black felt.

This is a very charming model. You might put it on your window-sill.

MATERIALS:

- Canvas
- Feathers
- Acrylic paint
- Material
- Coloured felt
- Scissors
- Glue
- Needle and cotton
- Ribbon
- Punch

INDIAN HEADDRESS

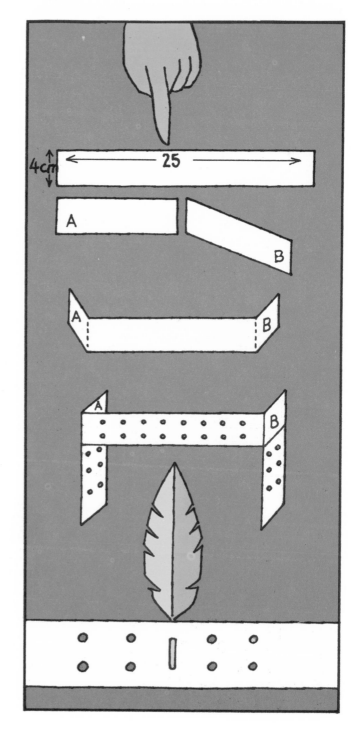

Cut two rectangles 25cm by 4cm out of canvas.

Cut one of them in half.

Fold the ends of the long piece 4cm from either end as shown.

Sew part A of the small rectangle on to part A of the large one. Sew part B of the small rectangle on to part B of the large one. Make holes as shown in the canvas with a punch.

Collect some feathers. Decorate them with acrylic paint or felt-tip pens. Leave to dry. Then push them through the holes as shown.

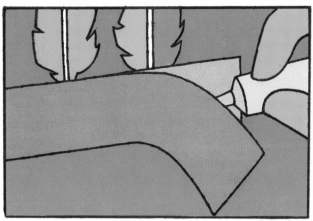

Cover the canvas with material, hiding the holes for the feathers.

Glue pieces of different coloured felts on to the material to make a pattern.

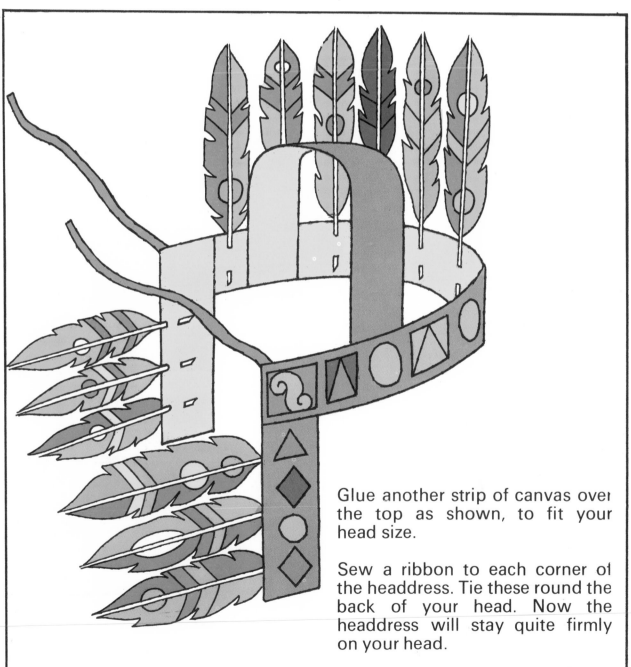

Glue another strip of canvas over the top as shown, to fit your head size.

Sew a ribbon to each corner of the headdress. Tie these round the back of your head. Now the headdress will stay quite firmly on your head.

MATERIALS:

- ● Strong card
- ● Pencil
- ● Scissors
- ● Material
- ● Pins
- ● Toy tennis racquet
- ● Old toothbrush
- ● Paint

SCREEN STENCIL

Draw a design on a piece of card. Cut it out so that you leave empty the shapes you want to print.

Get the paint, a toy tennis racquet and a toothbrush ready.

Place the material you want to print the design on over a table. Pin the pieces of card to the material.

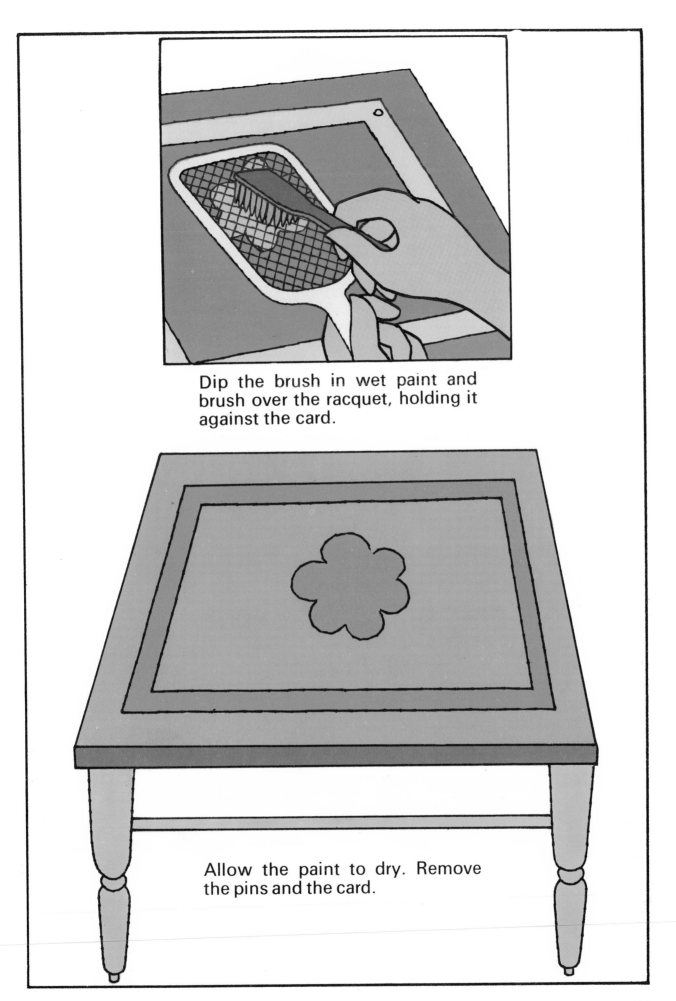

Dip the brush in wet paint and brush over the racquet, holding it against the card.

Allow the paint to dry. Remove the pins and the card.

SUN

Cut sixteen pieces of straw to the same length. Lay them across each other as shown, like rays of the sun.

Weave thread over and under alternate rays as shown.

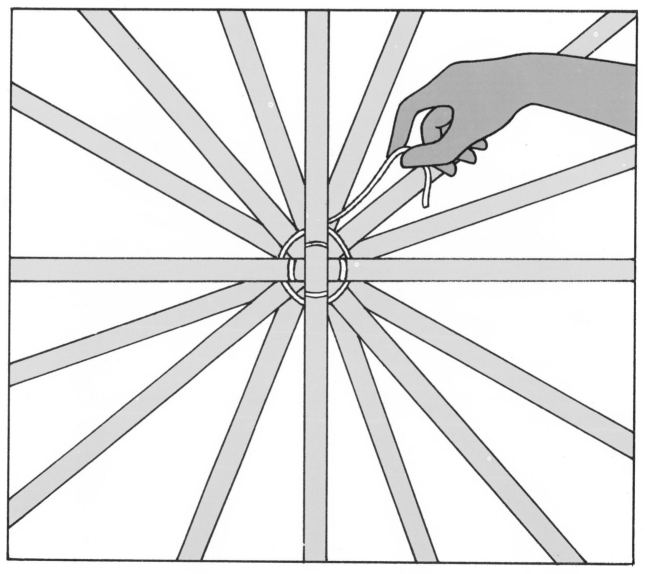

BAG

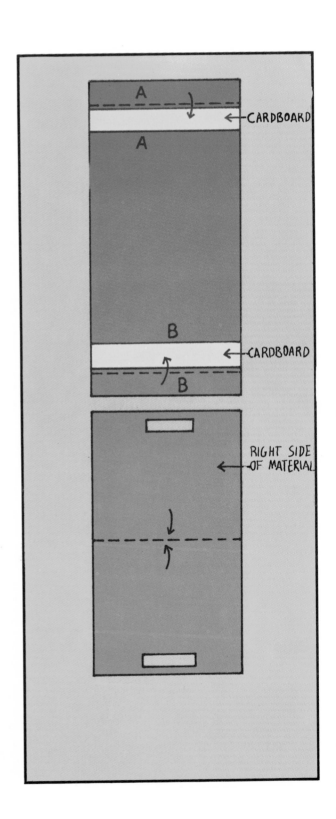

Cut a rectangle 1.1m by 34cm out of material (top picture).

Cut two strips of very flexible cardboard 5cm by 34cm. (shown in yellow).

Fold the material along the dotted lines in the direction of the arrows.

Glue A to A and B to B in the same way.

Cut out two rectangular slots though the material and the cardboard as shown (bottom picture). Then fold again in the direction of the arrows, with the right sides together.

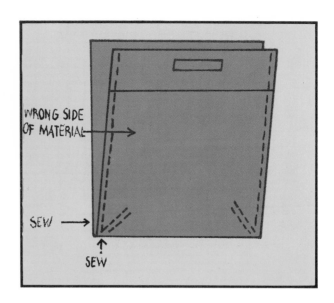

Sew up the sides and make darts as shown. Turn the bag the right way out.

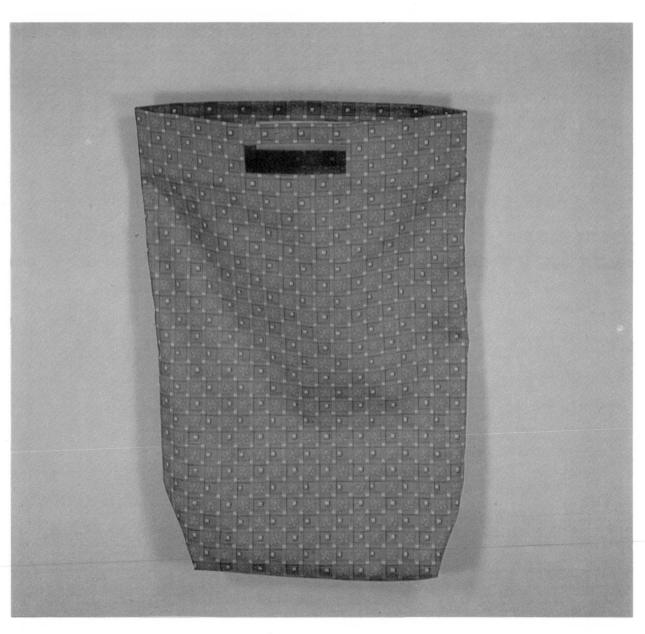

BOX

Take the box apart carefully as shown. Glue canvas to both sides of each piece.

Draw a design in pencil on one side only of each piece. Then fill in your designs with wool glued on to the canvas.

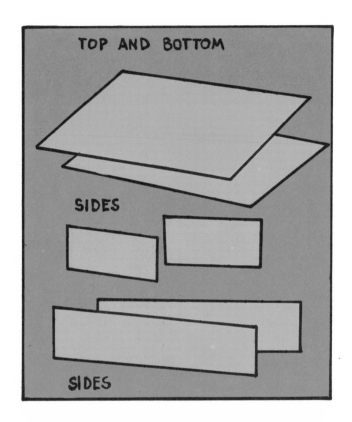

A design for the sides

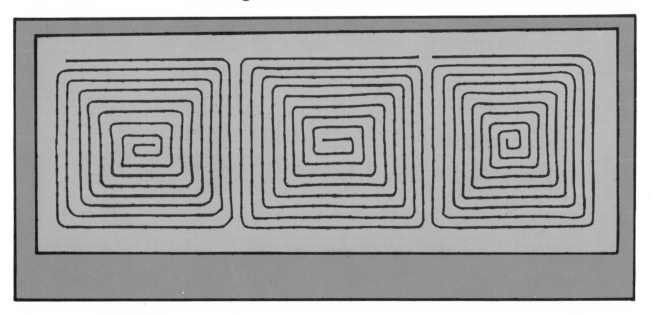

A design for the lid

When you have finished the decoration and the glue is dry, sew the box together again with small stitches.

BOOK MARKERS

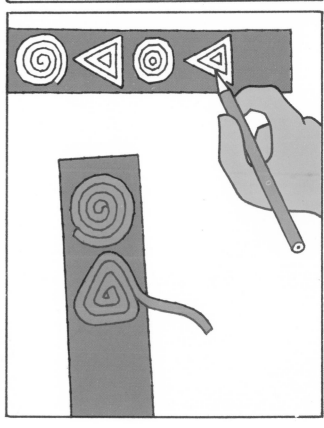

Cut some ribbons slightly longer than the size of the book you wish to mark. On each ribbon draw a simple pattern that you can repeat from top to bottom.

Glue strands of wool over the patterns as shown.

Sew the top ends of the ribbons together with wool.

Finish off the bottom ends by gluing on short pieces of wool to form fringes as in the photograph.

This multiple marker can mark different chapters in one book at the same time. You can make ties, decorate curtains etc. in the same way

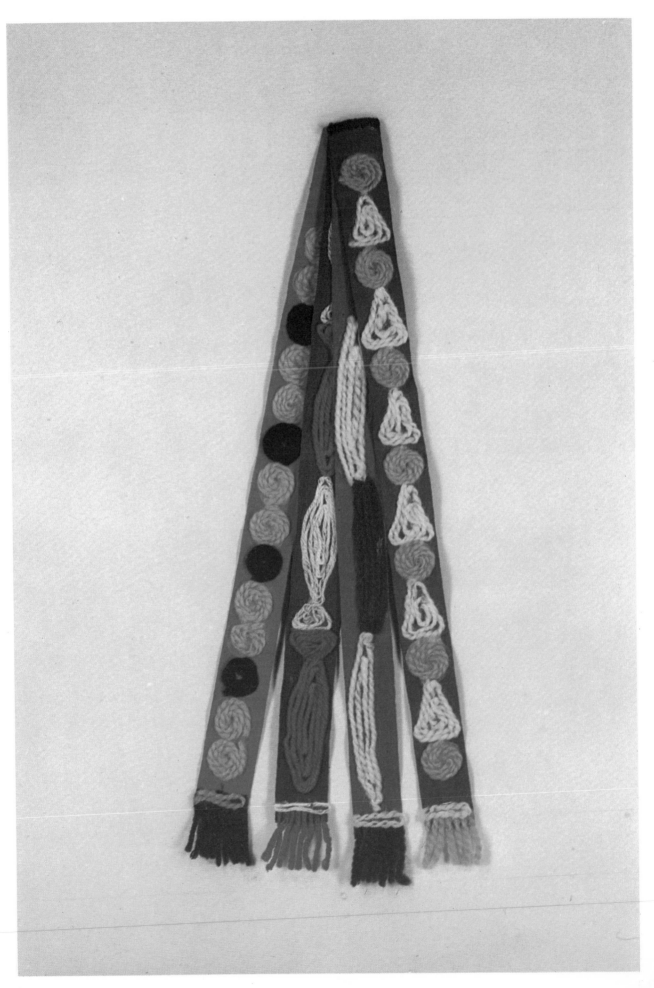

LAMPSHADE

Cut a rectangle out of card.

Spread glue over both sides of the rectangle and cover with canvas.

Trace the pattern shown on to the canvas.

Stick string along the lines of the pattern.

Glue the shorter end of the rectangle together.

Hang the lampshade from the ceiling with string as shown.

MATERIALS:

- Cardboard
- Pencil
- Wool
- Glue

BIRD MAT

Cut out a piece of cardboard as big as the mat you want to make.

Trace or draw your pictures on to the cardboard.

Now fill in the pictures and the background in your design. Use coloured wools that look nice together.

The picture below shows how to glue the wool on.

Try not to cut the wool until you have completely filled up the area you are using it for.

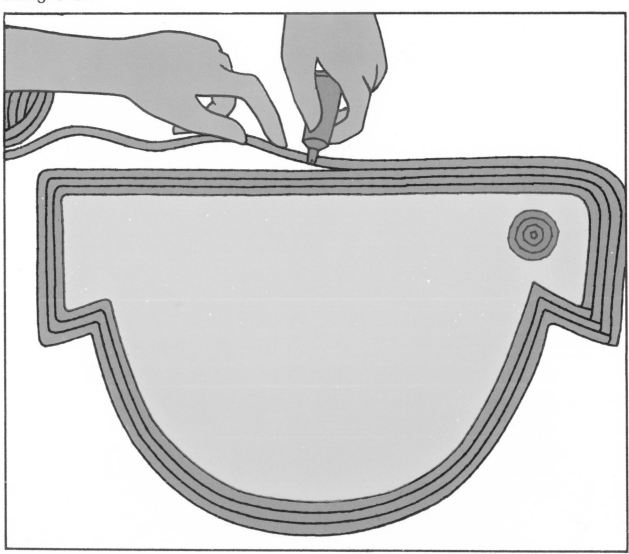

Once you have learnt this method, you can make lots of other things in the
same way.

DOVES

Use the same materials as on the previous page.

Draw the outlines of the doves on tracing paper and transfer the drawing to a piece of cardboard.

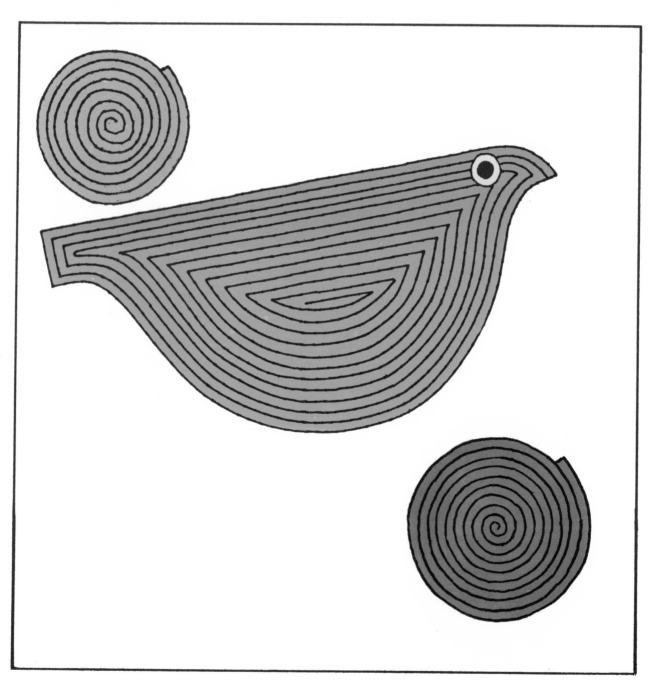

Glue wool round and round the outline of the doves. Repeat until all the spaces are filled in.

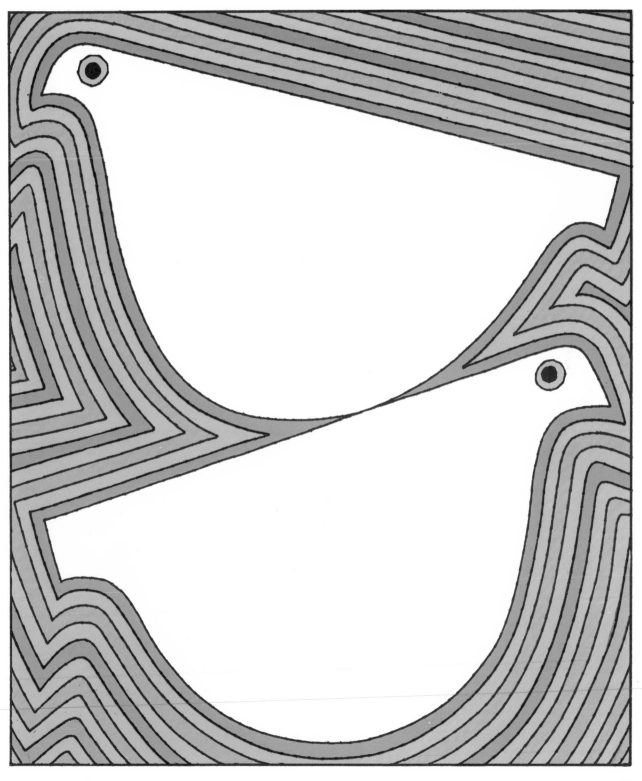

MATERIALS:

- Wool
- Pencil and paper
- Compasses
- Wool needle
- Scissors

WIG

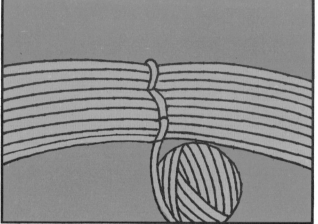

Cut strands of wool about 70cm long.

Use one of the strands to tie the others in the middle, three at a time.

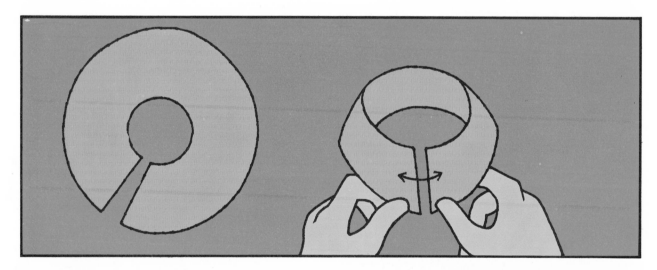

Draw and cut out the pattern above, first on paper and then on strong material the same colour as the wig. Sew the ends together.
This makes a skull cap on to which you put your wig.

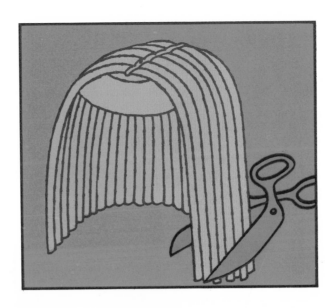

Sew the wig on to the skull cap with the same colour wool.
Trim the strands so that they hang tidily. Wear the wig loose or tie the wool in a pony tail with a bow.

DONKEY

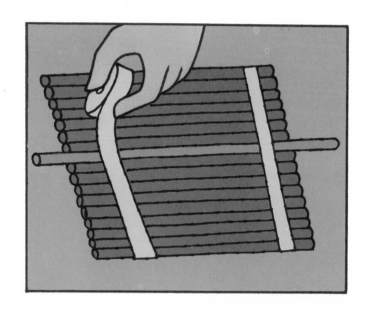

Cut the sticks into equal lengths except one longer one.

Lay the sticks next to each other. Stick a strip of sticky tape across either end as shown to make the body of the donkey. The long stick goes through the body to make the neck and tail. Make the sticks into a cylinder. Stick the ends together with tape.

The head is made in the same way as the body, only smaller. Pin two short sticks to the head for ears as shown.

Make the legs out of four more pieces of stick.

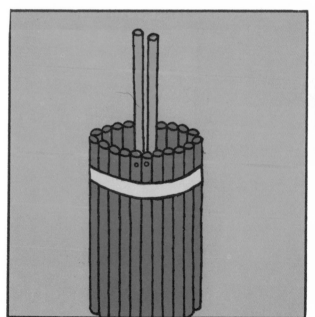

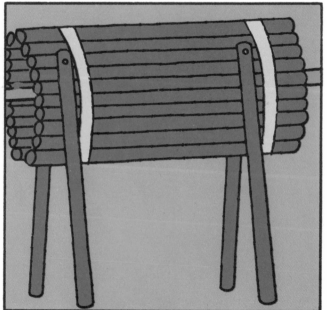

9

BUTTERFLIES

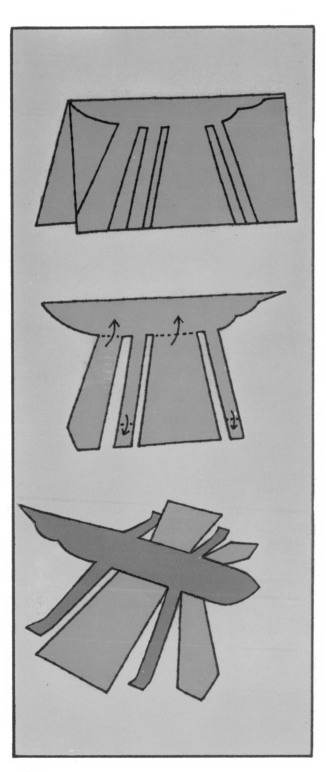

Cut out a piece of thin card. Fold it in half. Now draw on lines as shown on the left. Cut through both thicknesses of card along the lines.

Fold along the dotted lines in the direction of the arrows as shown.

Glue corduroy or velvet as shown (purple) along the parts that make the legs and the body.

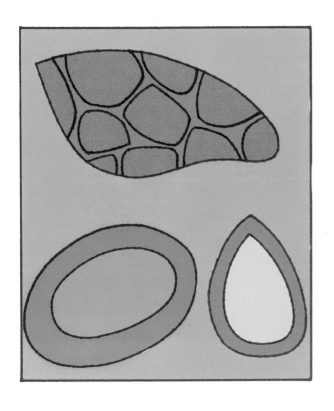

Cut wing shapes as shown on the left out of brightly coloured material. Glue on to the card wings. Put your butterflies in a cardboard box if you wish.

CUSHION

Cut out a rectangle of material. Fold in half, right sides together, and sew up the sides. Leave an opening for stuffing. Turn the right way out and stuff with wool etc.

You can cover both sides of the cushion or only one with crochet work as shown.

The cushion shown uses only one colour of wool. But you can use different colours if you wish.

Key to diagram below;
(.) a chain stitch
(I) a column stitch

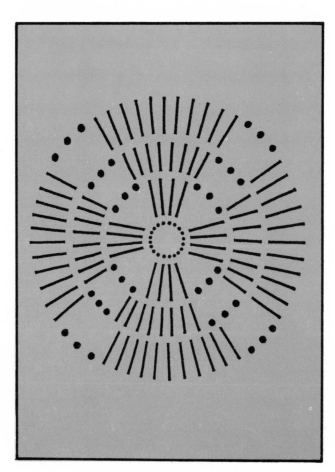

MATERIALS:

- **Felt in two colours**
- **Buttons**
- **Scissors**
- **Glue and cotton**
- **Tape measure**

FELT BELT

Measure your waist with the tape measure. Cut a band of felt 6cm wide, long enough to go round your waist.

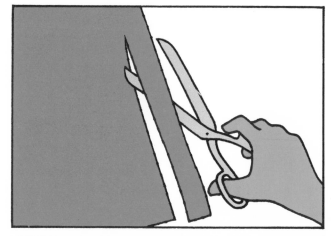

Take another colour of felt and make two strips 12cm longer than the first strip each only 1cm wide.

Glue these two strips along the felt base as shown, half a centimeter from the edges. The extra 12cm should project at one end only.

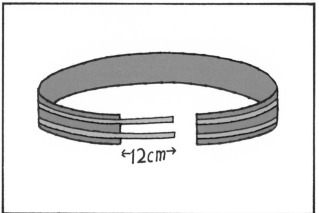

At the other end, where the thin strips meet the end of the belt, sew four buttons on each of the thin strips, 3cm between each button as shown.

Cut four buttonholes in each of the thin projecting strips, leaving 3cm between each buttonhole.

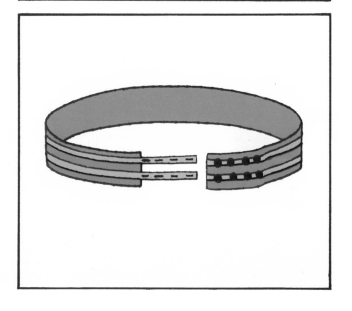

134

The belt shown is of red felt, the thin strips are blue and the buttons are black. Work out other colour combinations to match the dresses you wear.

MATERIALS:

- Board to work on
- Pencil
- Scissors
- Thin card
- Brush
- Acrylic paint
- Pins
- Material for printing on

PRINTING
ON MATERIAL

Draw the outline of a design on a piece of thin card. Cut it out.

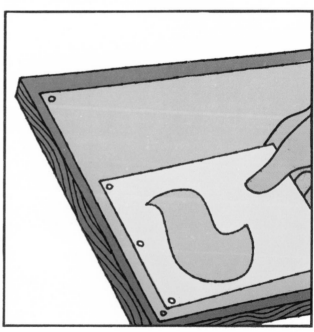

Put the material you are going to print on a board.
Pin the card stencil on top of it as shown.

Prepare acrylic paint or a fabric dye, and a square-ended paintbrush.

Paint over the hole in the card-board.

Allow the paint to dry. Remove the pins and the card, leaving the printed material. Repeat as many times as necessary.

BIRD

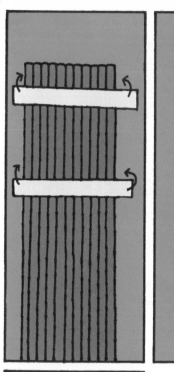

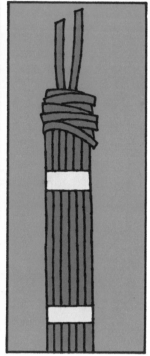

Cut a handful of sticks the same length. Lay them side by side.

Stick them all together with two pieces of adhesive tape as shown. Roll into a cylinder so that the ends of the adhesive tape stick together.

Wind a piece of stick round the top end to form the bird's head.

For the tail, make holes in each piece of stick with a thick needle. Thread another thin stick through the holes.

The wings are made of sticks going through the body, opening out like a fan in the same way as the tail.

Join the body to the wings with pins or tape.

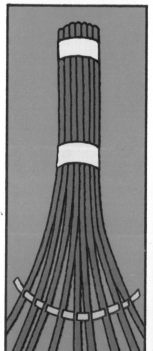

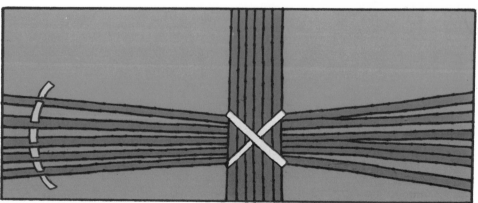

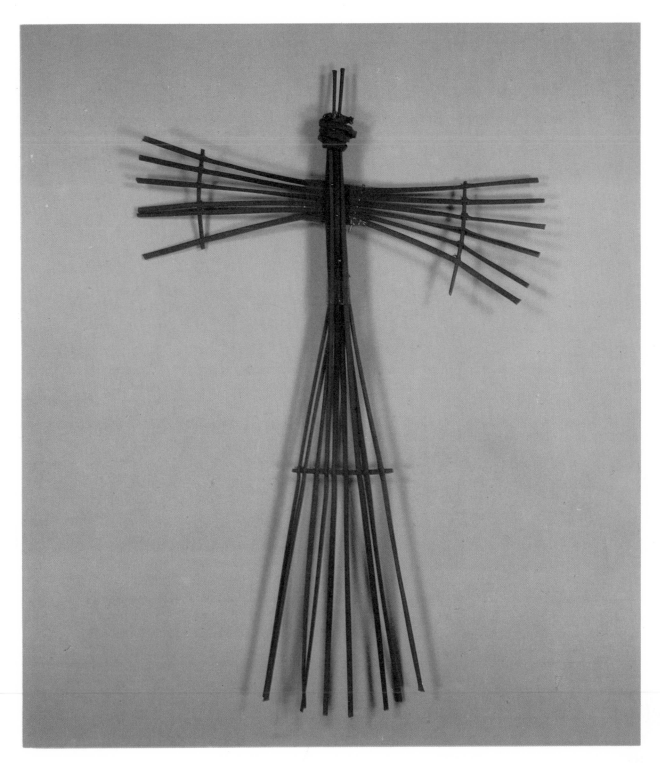

MATERIALS:

● Cardboard
● Coloured
  paper
● Raffia
● Scissors
● Glue

SMALL RAFFIA BASKET

Draw the shape on the right on a piece of cardboard. Cut it out.

Take some coloured paper and cut out a five-sided shape B, for the bottom. Glue on the cardboard over area B.

Bend the sides up.

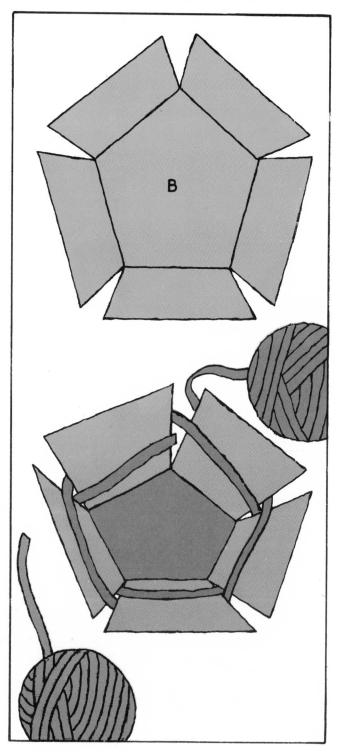

Make up two balls of raffia in different colours.

Thread the raffia of one colour round the front of one side, behind the next and so on, until you have been right round twice.
Do the same with the second ball of raffia.
Continue alternating the two colours until you reach the top.

Finish off the top of the basket by gluing on wide pieces of raffia or coloured paper as shown. This should be the same colour as the paper on the bottom, or the raffia used on the sides.

MATERIALS:

● Cardboard
● Scissors
● Glue
● String
● Transparent paper
● Pencil

BIRD

In the following pages, you will find a series of projects using string as the basic material. The first is a bird.

To make the bird, trace round the design shown on the left on tracing paper, and transfer to the cardboard.

Now cut round the outline on the cardboard.

Glue the string along the lines of the design as shown.

ANGEL

The materials used are the same as on the previous page.

The method used is the same too. Trace the drawing of the angel on tracing paper and transfer it to the cardboard.

Cut the cardboard round the outline. Glue the string along the lines of the drawing.

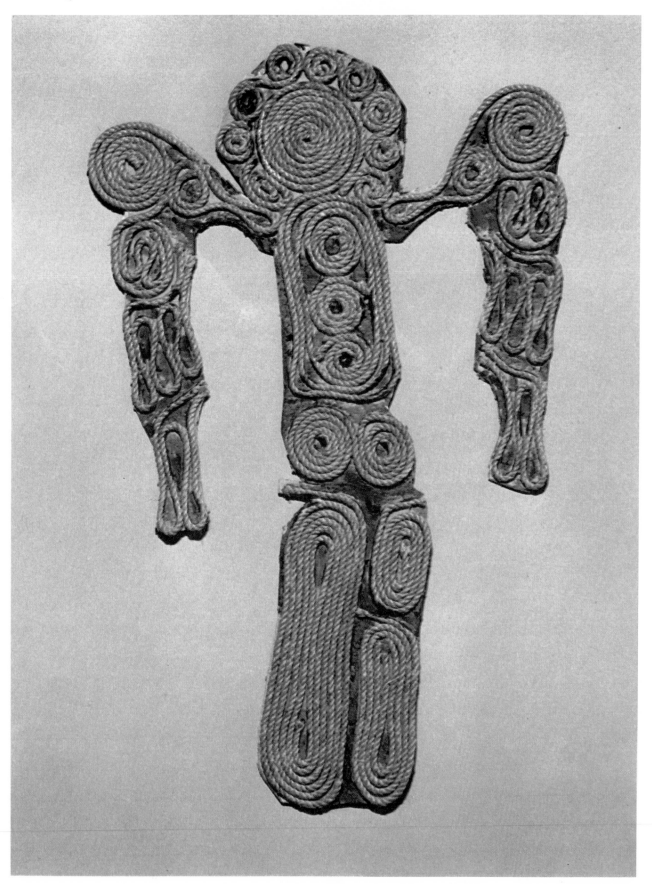

10

TARGET

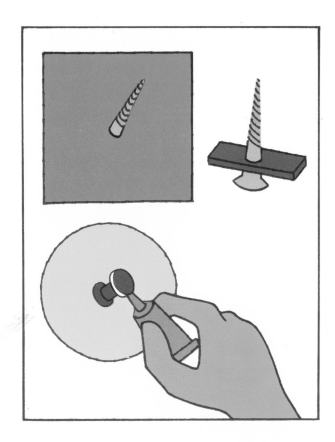

Cut out a square piece of cardboard.
Screw the screw through a piece of wood as shown on the right. Now push the screw through the middle of the cardboard square. Glue down the wood on the back to make sure that the screw is firmly fixed.

Cut out a circle of cardboard as shown, rather smaller than the square.
Stick a cotton reel in the middle of the circle.

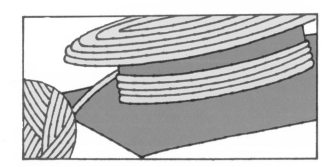

Decorate the square on the side where the point of the screw sticks out, and the side of the circle without the reel by sticking on circles of wool as shown in the big photograph.

Wind a long piece of wool round the reel, and finish off with a tassel.

Place the screw into the hole in the reel. Lay the whole thing on a flat surface. Pull the tassel out quickly and then let go. The whirling colours will look very pretty.

Mount the design on a wall as a decoration.

MATERIALS:

- Card
- Canvas
- Glue
- Felt-tip pens
- Materials
- Wool
- Scissors

BOTTLE COVER

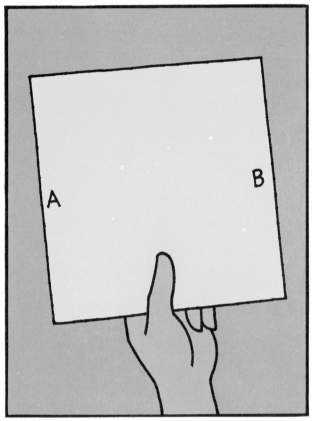

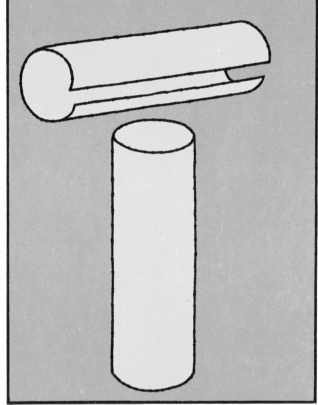

Cut a square or rectangle out of thin card. The size you need depends on the size of the bottle. Glue canvas to the card to cover it completely on the outside.

Make a tube by gluing side B to A as shown.

This is how you start all the designs for bottle covers shown on the

following pages, and lots of others you should be able to make up yourself.

Every design shown uses wool, felt or tartan decoration. Some also need felt-tip pens.

The page opposite shows the easiest way to make a top for the bottle covers.

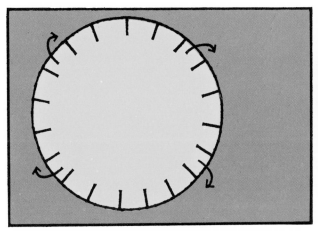

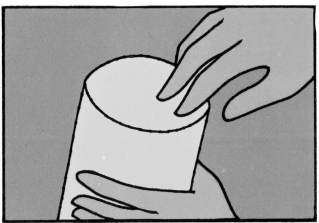

Cut a circle 10cm in diameter. Make a few short cuts round the edge as shown. Bend the flaps down and stick them inside the top rim of the tube. Stick canvas over the top.

The bottle cover shown is decorated with wool stuck to the canvas in half-circles.

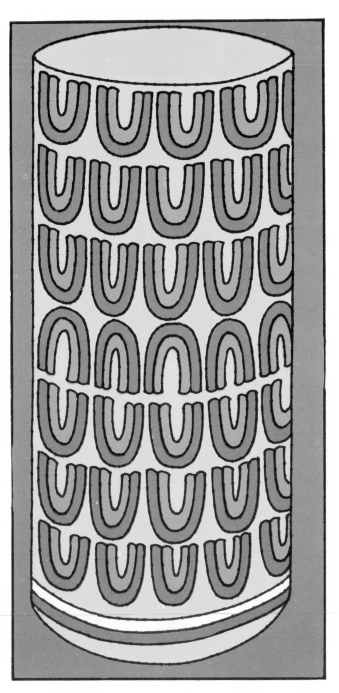

BOTTLE COVER

These bottle covers are made in the same way as the one on the previous page. The materials used are also the same.

The decoration can be different. The design below is done with thick felt-tip pens.
The beret is made of material stuck over the top.

Make a tube of thin card as shown on the previous page. Cut a piece of canvas the same size as the card.
Draw parallel lines on the outside of the canvas in pencil. Stick the canvas to the card.

Cut several equal-sized circles out of brown felt. Cut them in half and stick them to the canvas, as shown in the photograph, on either side of the lines you have drawn.

BOTTLE COVER

This bottle cover looks like a Scotsman.
Make a tube of thin card. Cover it with canvas. Cut the various parts of the clothing from different pieces of material. Stick these to the canvas as in the picture. Add final details to the model in felt-tip pens.

CAP

Cut two circles out of tartan material as used for the kilt. The diameter should be about 6cm more than that of the cylinder.

Sew round the two circles with the right sides together.

Cut out a hole in the middle of only one of the circles, slightly smaller than the tube. Turn the cap the right way out.

Make cuts round the edge of the inner circle as shown. Bend the flaps outwards. Fix the cap to the bottle cover by sticking the flaps to the outside top rim of the tube. Now cover these flaps with a ribbon.

Complete the cap with a pompom (for instructions, see page 46).

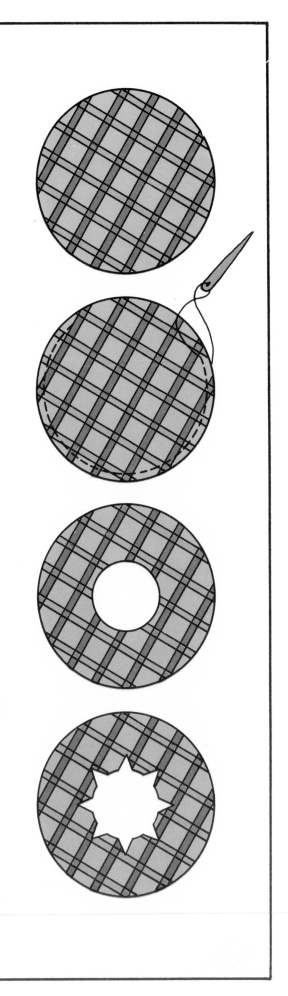

MATERIALS:

- Coloured felt
- Wire
- Needle and cotton
- Scissors
- Card

PENNANTS

Cut a rectangle out of felt. Fold over the top edge and sew along the dotted line. Push a wire through the loop and bend round the ends.

Make up any patterns you like for your pennants.

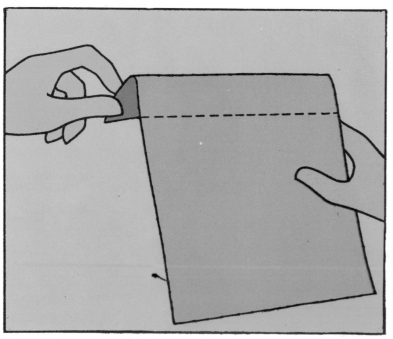

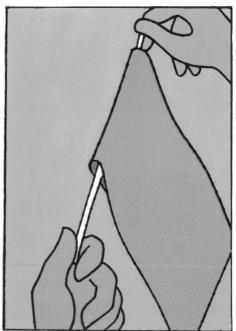

Cut the bits of the pattern out of card first, and then out of felt. Now stick them on to the pennant.

If you tie a cord to the ends of the wire, you can hang the pennant on your wall.

You can see two designs for pennants in the photograph opposite.

MATERIALS:

- 4-ply wool in different colours
- Crochet hook
- Needle
- Cotton

BEDCOVER

This bedcover is made out of six-sided shapes (hexagons) in crochet. Make each hexagon as follows:

1. Make six chain stitches and join together with a slip stitch.

2. Three column stitches (III) two chain stitches (..) three column stitches, two chain stitches, and so on.

3. As shown in the diagram.

Sew the hexagons together with small stitches on the wrong side of the crochet work.

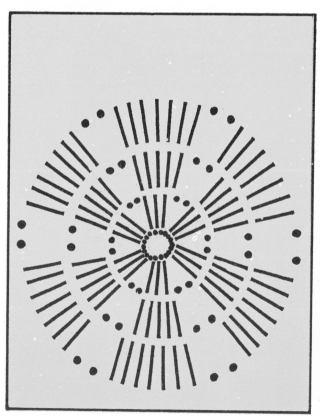

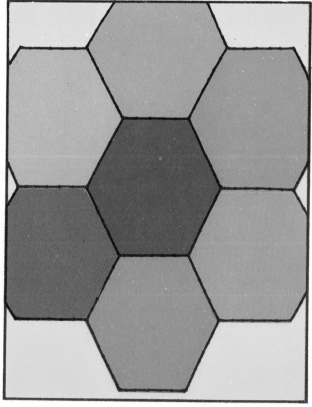

The number of hexagons you need depends on the size of the bed and the thickness of the wool and the crochet hook.

Finish off the cover with a fringe (see page 44).

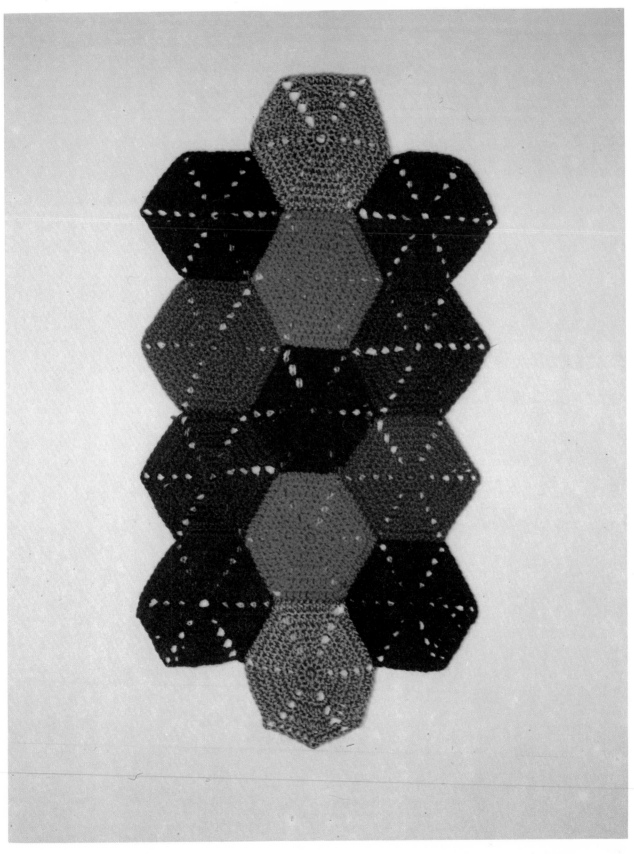

BOOK COVERS

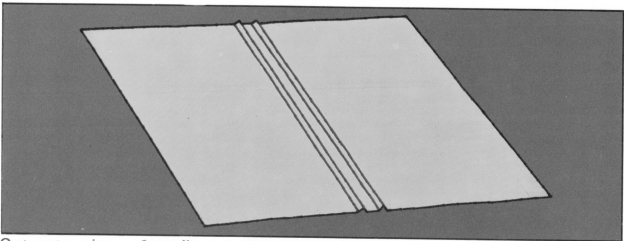

Cut out a piece of cardboard slightly larger than whole outside surface of the book you wish to cover.

Make some creases down the centre of the cardboard as shown above so that it will bend easily.

Cut out a piece of material larger than the cardboard and glue it to the cardboard and round the edges as shown.

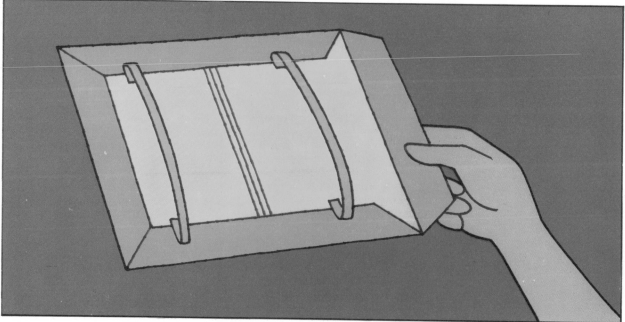

Sew another rectangle of material on the inside of the cover as above.

Sew on two strips of elastic to the inside top and bottom, as shown. These will hold the existing covers of the book.

If you have used a plain material for your cover, you can decorate it with other bits of coloured materials or with felt-tip pens.

LITTLE RED RIDING HOOD PUPPET

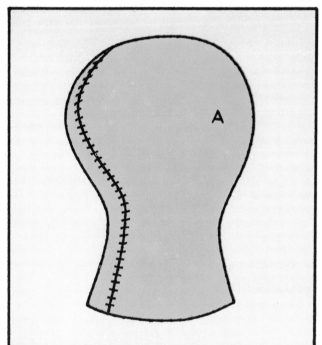

HEAD:
Cut shape A out of three pieces of felt placed on top of each other.

Sew the three pieces together with small stitches, to form the round head of your puppet.

Stuff tight with cotton cloth.

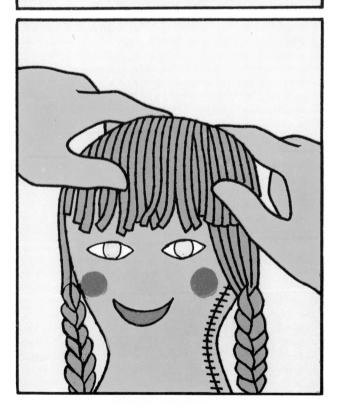

Stick on little pieces of coloured felt for the mouth and eyes. Paint in the cheeks and nose with a red felt-tip pen.

Stick pieces of wool on to the head to form a fringe. Make two plaits from the same colour wool and stick them on each side of the head.

160

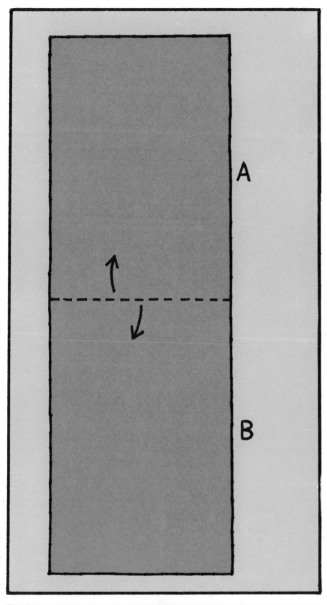

This is the pattern for the puppet's hood. It is made of red velvet. Fold it in half and sew edges A and B together.

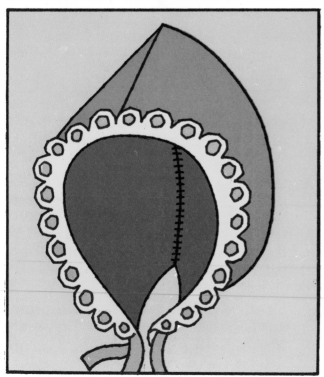

You can finish off the hood with a frill round the face. Add a thin ribbon and tie in a bow at the bottom.

11

PUPPET DRESSES

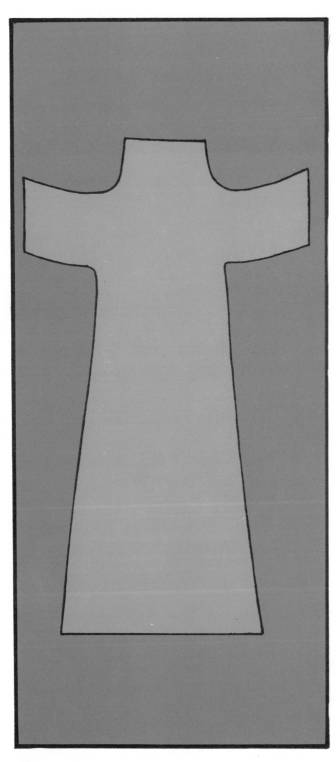

CLOTHES:

The pattern on the left can be used for all the puppets. The front and the back are exactly the same.

Sew the front, and back pieces together leaving the collar open for the head to be sewn on. Leave the ends of the sleeves open for the hands, and the bottom open for your hand.

Dresses can be made from different kinds and colours of material. Make them suit your puppet as on the following pages.

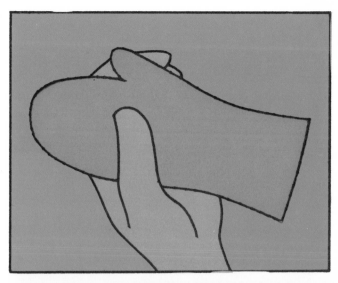

HANDS:

The pattern for the hands is also the same for all three following puppets.

Cut four pieces like this for each puppet. Each hand is made from two pieces sewn together and stuffed with cotton.

GRANNY PUPPET

GRANNY'S HEAD:

Cut shape A out of two pieces of felt.

Cut shape B out of the same felt.

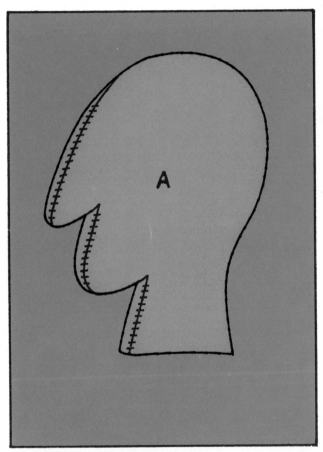

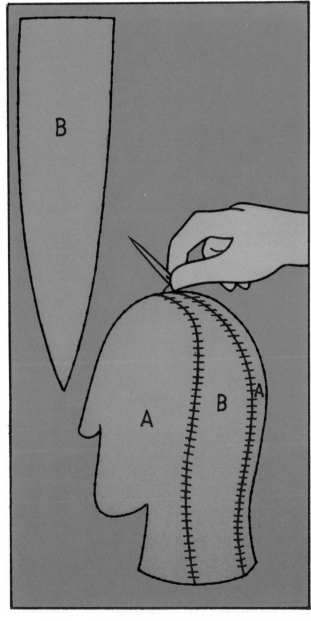

Place shape B between the two shapes A. Sew together with small stitches. Stuff with cotton and sew up.

Decorate the head with grey wool and different coloured felt. Make spectacles from wire.

WOLF PUPPET

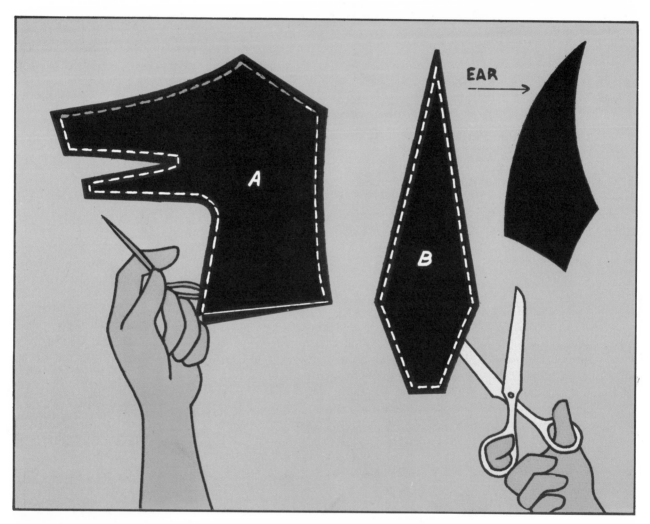

WOLF'S HEAD:

Cut two shapes A out of black felt. Sew them together along the white dotted lines, except for the top of the nose and the top of the head.

Cut out shape B and sew it to the open top parts of the other two pieces, with the point at the tip of the nose.
Stuff with cotton cloth.

Each ear is made out of a piece of black felt as shown on the right of the picture above. Sew to the top of the head.

MATERIALS:

- Thin card
- Black, white and green felt
- Glue
- Wide elastic
- Scissors

MASK

Cut two circles about 17cm in diameter out of card.

Cut two more in the same size out of black felt. Glue these to the card.

Cut out two green felt circles about 15cm in diameter. Cut out an eye shape as shown on the right in the middle of each one. Glue the outside green bits on to the middle of the black felt circles.

Cut out a piece of white felt the same shape as the inside bits of green felt, but slightly smaller. Glue these inside the green bits on to the black circles.

Glue a little black felt circle in the middle of the white shape.

Glue more black pieces as shown on the right on to the green felt.

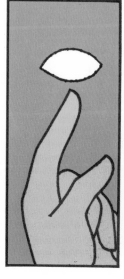

Make a circle of elastic to fit round your head. Glue the front of the elastic as shown to the back of the card and felt circles.

If you make little holes to look through, you can wear the mask as shown.

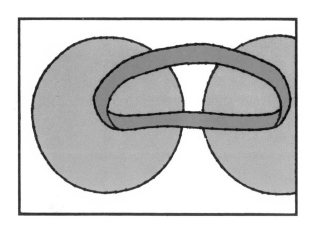

BAG

Cut a rectangle 30cm by 60cm out of canvas for the lining of the bag.

Cut eighteen squares 12cm by 12cm out of different coloured materials. Sew them together three across as shown with seams 1cm wide on the wrong side of the material.

Cut two double strips of canvas for the handles.

Sew the lining to the rectangle of different coloured materials you have already sewn together.

Fold the rectangle in half with the lining on the outside. Sew along the dotted lines and turn the whole bag the right way out.

170

MATERIALS:

- Cardboard box
- Thin card
- Orange paper
- Scissors
- Glue
- String
- Pencil

ELEPHANT

The following pages show you how to make a series of animals out of cardboard boxes. The first one is an elephant.

Cover the box with orange paper.

Draw in pencil the patterns shown below and opposite for each part of the covered box.

Glue the string along the lines of the patterns. Make the ears out of spirals of string glued to the sides of the head.

FACE

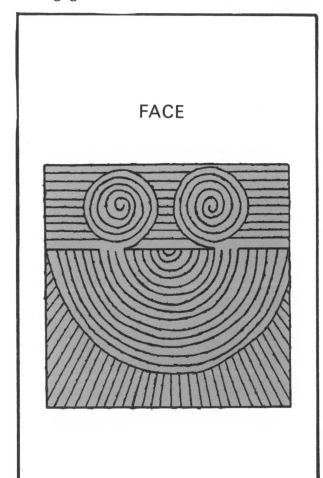

BACK

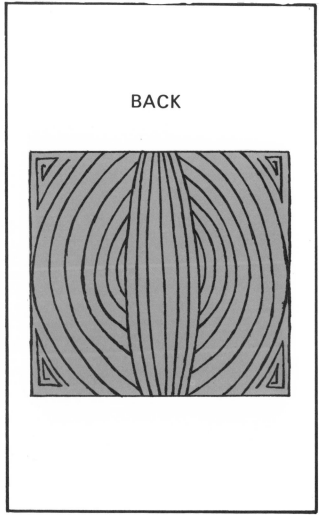

SIDES

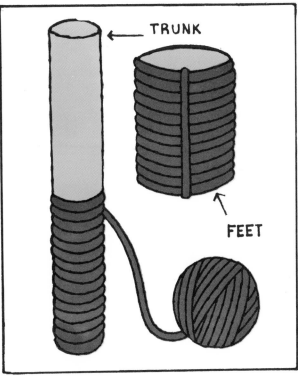

TRUNK

FEET

The feet and the trunk are made from rectangles of cardboard rolled into tubes as shown, and then covered with string.

LION AND COCK

MATERIALS:

- Cardboard box
- Coloured paper
- Card
- Scissors
- Cardboard
- String
- Glue
- Wire
- Pencil

To make the lion, start with a cardboard box as before. Cover with coloured paper.

Draw on the design shown, in pencil. Stick string along the lines of the design.

The legs are small tubes of card covered with string.

The ears are string spirals glued to the head.

For the tail, cut three or four pieces of string, join with a knot and glue to the body of the lion as shown.

To make the cock, cover another box with coloured paper.

Draw the design for each part of the box in pencil. Stick string along the lines of the design.
The neck of the cock is made of a tube of card.
The legs and feet are made of wire wound round with string.

Make the tail out of four more pieces of wire wound round with string.
The crest, head and beak are also made of string and wire, and stuck to the body.

RECORD CASE

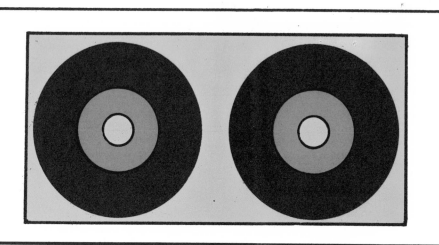

Cut out a rectangle out of cardboard, as shown, slightly larger than two records side by side.

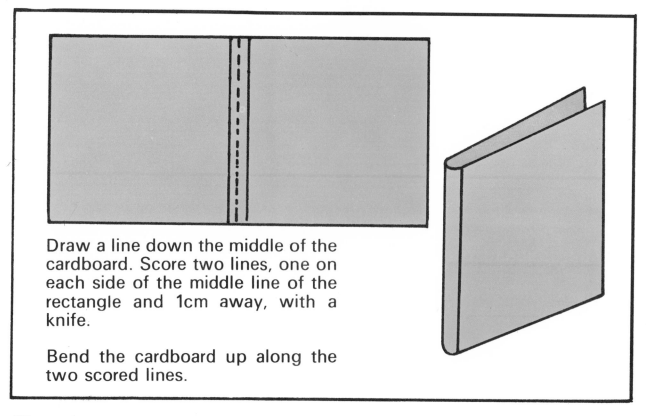

Draw a line down the middle of the cardboard. Score two lines, one on each side of the middle line of the rectangle and 1cm away, with a knife.

Bend the cardboard up along the two scored lines.

Open out the cardboard again. Cut out two pieces of canvas the same size as the cardboard.
Glue these on either side of the cardboard.

Cut another piece of canvas, shown below in red. As you can see this is shorter in one direction than the cardboard, but longer the other way. Glue this to the cardboard, making pleats on the inside, as shown.

Make a canvas flap if possible with a press-stud as shown, to close the case.

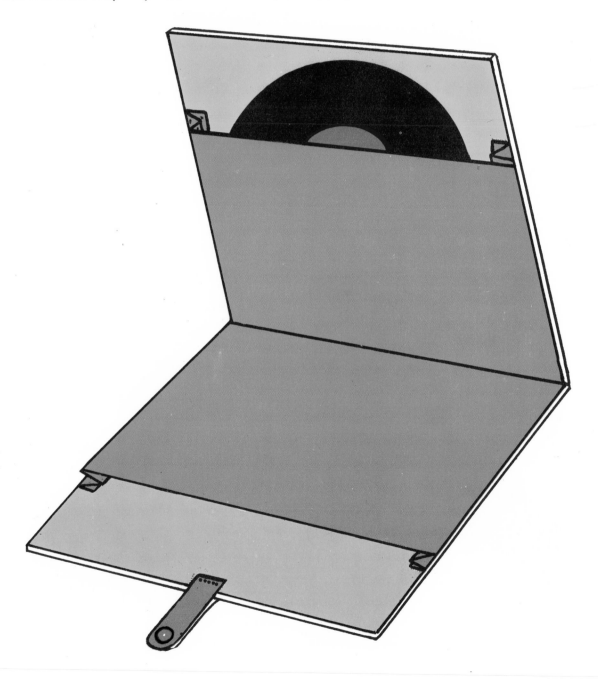

- Compasses
- Ruler
- Pencil
- Coloured wools
- Glue

DECORATING THE RECORD CASE

Here you can see one way of decorating the record case shown on the previous pages.

Draw a circle 12cm in diameter on to canvas. Draw in the diameter PH. Divide this into six equal parts, marked A,B,C,D, and E on the picture.

Put the point of your compasses on A, the pencil (or nib) on B, and draw a semicircle from P to B.

Now put the point on B, the pencil on D, and draw a semicircle from D to P.

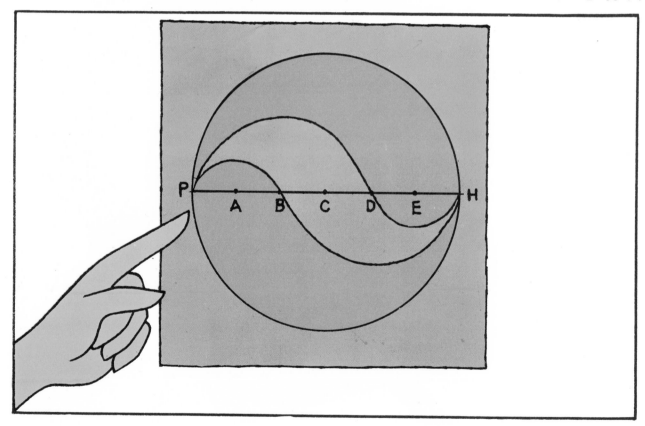

Now make D the centre of a semicircle underneath, from B to H.
Finally make E the centre of a semicircle from D to H, all as shown.

Fill in the central 'S' shape as shown below by gluing down pieces of mauve wool.
Fill in the rest of the circle with white wool.

Fill in the remaining space with red wool.

You can repeat the same pattern on the other side of the case, or make up a new one.

MATERIALS:

- Cardboard
- Scissors
- Canvas
- Glue
- String
- Pencil
- Needle and strong cotton

HEN

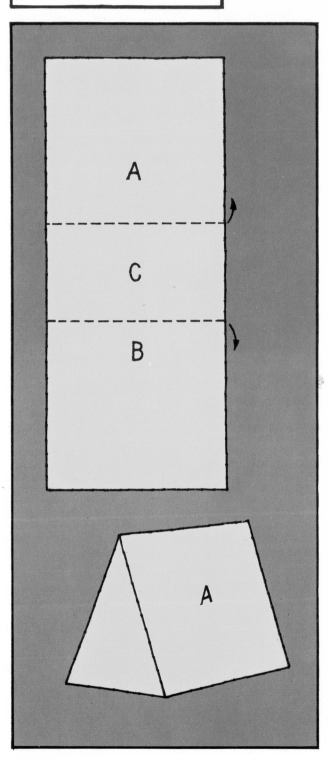

Cut out a cardboard rectangle 40cm by 15cm.

Fold this along the dotted lines shown on the left, in the direction of the arrows.
Area C forms the bottom of the model.

Cut out two cardboard triangles to fit the holes at the front and back of the model.

Cover all three pieces of cardboard with canvas and decorate as follows:

Trace the designs shown on the opposite page on to the corresponding pieces.

Sew the pieces together with small stitches and strong thread.

Finally, glue string along the lines of the design.
The tail, beak and crest can be made by gluing on string shapes as in the photograph.

INDEX